25 TROPICAL HOUSES
in Indonesia

AMIR SIDHARTA

introduction by AMANDA ACHMADI

photographs by MASANO KAWANA

with assistance from REITA MALAON

PERIPLUS

Published by Periplus Editions, with
editorial offices at 130 Joo Seng Road
#06-01/03, Singapore 368357.

Text © 2006 Periplus Editions (HK) Ltd
Photographs © 2006 Masano Kawana

ISBN 0 7946 0245 2
Printed in Singapore

Distributed by:
Asia Pacific
Berkeley Books Pte Ltd, 130 Joo Seng
Road #06-01/03, Singapore 368357.
Tel: (65) 6280 1330; Fax: (65) 6280 6290
E-mail: inquiries@periplus.com.sg
http://www.periplus.com

PT Java Books Indonesia
Kawasan Industri Pulogadung,
Jl. Rawa Gelam IV No. 9,
Jakarta 13930, Indonesia
Tel: (021) 4682 1088
Fax: (021) 461 0207
Email: cs@javabooks.co.id

*North America, Latin America
and Europe*
Tuttle Publishing, 364 Innovation Drive,
North Clarendon, Vermont 05759, USA.
Tel: (802) 773 8930; Fax: (802) 773 6993
E-mail: info@tuttlepublishing.com
http://www.tuttlepublishing.com

Japan
Tuttle Publishing, Yaekari Building, 3F,
5-4-12 Osaki, Shinagawa-ku, Tokyo
141-0032. Tel: (813) 5437 0171;
Fax: (813) 5437 0755
E-mail: tuttle-sales@gol.com

09 08 07 06
6 5 4 3 2 1

Endpapers Left: Rino & Sarah Residence,
Pondok Indah, Jakarta (page 36), architect
Yori Antar; Right: Inke Gallery House,
Menteng, Jakarta (page 176), designer
Yusman Siswandi.

Page 1 Solo Home, Kebayoran Baru,
Jakarta (page 54), designer Jaya Ibrahim.

Page 2 Permata Villa, Permata Hijau,
Jakarta (page 84), architect Andra Matin.

Pages 4–5 Setiadharma House, Pondok
Indah, Jakarta (page 210), architect
Kusuma Agustianto.

Pages 6–7 Permata Villa, Permata Hijau,
Jakarta (page 84), architect Andra Matin;
Tirtawisata House, Permata Buana
(page 166), architects Antony Liu & Ferry
Ridwan; Rino & Sarah Residence, Pondok
Indah, Jakarta (page 36), architect Yori
Antar.

contents

the quest for a new tropical architecture

For most people, the words "tropics" and "tropical architecture" conjure up images of a lush landscape illuminated by the tropical sun and dotted with "quaint" or "exotic" buildings. While such notions have largely been popularized by the region's tourism industry, inside tropical Indonesia itself architecture has always been influenced by constantly shifting phenomena, in particular its multifaceted society, a complex classical and modern history, extreme disparities between wealth and poverty, a legacy of colonial occupation, and dynamic economic development which has triggered rapid movements of people away from their traditional environments and communities.

Living in the tropics is much more than living in a hot, humid climate or in a lush, green environment. It involves constant negotiation between traditional ways of life, the forces of nature, and the advance of modernization, including the latest international style trends. In Indonesia, this negotiation is marked by a range of contradictions: an ideal natural setting versus dense residential areas; a comfortable temperature versus an unbearable combination of humidity, heavy downpours, and pollution; indigenous (vernacular) houses and colonial architectural legacies versus towering American-style apartment blocks; and gated housing enclaves versus marginalized slums. Added to this mix are an often-volatile political environment, erratic economic development, a socially and economically polarized society, and uncontrolled and unplanned urbanization.

Emerging from the depths of these contradictions is a rapidly growing upper middle and upper class operating in a dynamic and plural urban culture. The houses featured in this book provide insights into the aspirations of these two affluent groups—aspirations that embrace new styles of living, changing family patterns and activities, cross-cultural networking, and variations in work practices—all of which demand innovative and inspiring architectural solutions. This is an exciting development, one that has long been overshadowed by the country's traditional systems of social privilege and by the packaging of Indonesian "cultural" and "modern" identities through colonial history and periods of nation building.[1] In such a changing and challenging milieu, the country's "tropical architecture" needs to be seen as much more than nostalgic, picturesque images of the exotic tropics or as scientific solutions to the control of climate.[2]

Nostalgic, picturesque images of tropical architecture in Indonesia have been, and still are, largely a figment of the imagination of people outside the region. Driven by Orientalist notions of tropical Asia as an ever-peaceful, finite, harmonious, and exotic place, and by current tourist aspirations for an old-fashioned and non-Western living experience, tropical

Right Lush tropical "fountain" grass not only filters views and light into the living room of the Tirtawisata House (page 166), but also camouflages the roof of the garage on which it is planted and provides a touch of green against the house's stark planar walls.

Above Creative interpretations of
vernacular building traditions are
evident in the play on opacity and
transparency in the Rino & Sarah
Residence (page 36), exemplified
by the "house on stilts" facade and
the study at the back cantilevered
over the swimming pool.

architecture in Indonesia is romanticized as a set of building forms that harmoniously blend with a tropical green landscape—a symbolic scenic paradise or an exotic escape from the rat race of modern urban living.[3] Moreover, in contrast to architectural developments in the West, the architectural style of tropical Indonesia is often envisaged as ideal and finite rather than complex and evolving, an amalgam of centuries-old traditions and influences.

In exclusive resorts and other tourist areas, indigenous or vernacular architectural traditions are widely considered the main source of inspiration. Reproduced outside their immediate socio-geographical contexts, transformed into élite icons, and reduced to aesthetic expressions in order to satisfy tourist desires for the "exotic," they often overshadow our understanding of the actual challenges of housing in modern Indonesia.[4] Moreover, what used to be ethnically identifiable communities spread throughout the country have been gradually transformed into a heterogeneous and mostly urban society. Against this background, an ethnically specific vernacular architecture has limited relevance as it faces new demands for privacy, dynamic communal and economic activities, and a variety of architectural expressions. Rather, contemporary Indonesian architects need to creatively embrace and cultivate the most suitable aspects of vernacular concepts while responding to transformations of place and changing notions of community.

The second approach to the country's "tropical architecture style"—climatic-responsive and typological design—has explored diverse methods of responding to the hot, humid climate through the employment of such devices as sun screens, louvers, ventilation systems, and heat insulation. It has also identified a set of building materials and building forms, including the courtyard house, terrace house, and detached or semi-detached house, as suitable living contexts for the tropics. This approach is important since it explores natural ways of coping with the climate as opposed to artificial techniques, which are often environmentally flawed. But it can also unconsciously reduce tropical architecture to predictable building forms and details. Rather than being seen as an innovative exploration of problem solving and spatiality, architectural design becomes a pastiche of preconceived solutions and forms.

The concept of regionalism has also entered the discourse on tropical architecture. Proponents assert the need for contemporary architects to promote distinct cultural and geographical forms in the face of globalization and the rapid spread of capitalism, exemplified by the pervasive spread of International Style architecture and Western building technology.[5] It is suggested that the cultural uniqueness and varying climatic conditions of each region can drive regional architectural differences.[6] But the search for regional architectural differences should not become an obsession to create a local architecture that is the antithesis of the modern West, but one in tune with the potential and challenge of living in the region.[7]

Envisioning tropical architecture beyond the two predominant approaches is critical in today's Indonesia. The country cannot be content with a particular architectural image. Against a background of pervasive urban drift, architects will inevitably have to turn their talents towards the making of sustainable tropical cities. Outside the realm of élite classical kingdom capitals, Indonesia has had little experience in managing its present pattern of urbanization—the so-called "megacity" phenomenon. In contrast, Western experiences of urbanization have emerged from different historical processes. As such, Western notions of urbanization cannot address those challenges faced by Asian cities.[8] New architectural strategies for tropical Indonesia need to tackle the challenges of the country's rapid urbanization.

This book is a window on contemporary explorations of living in the tropics as experienced by modern Indonesians, a different realm from the well-published architectural experiences of expatriates and tourists. To understand the background to these explorations in relation to the twenty-five houses featured in this book, it is necessary to turn to past experiments with tropical architecture in Indonesia.

The Diverse Faces of Tropical Architecture in Indonesia

Tropical architecture is not a contemporary concept or creation. In Indonesia, tropicalization of architectural design has been widely articulated during different periods of the country's history as attempts were made to construct an Indonesian identity. At certain times, tropicalization of architecture has been translated as a set of formulaic building forms and complementary climatic devices; at other times, it has been envisaged at the conceptual level of form making. From indigenous dwelling units to colonial-style bungalow residences, from state-sponsored housing complexes to exclusive real estate housing enclaves, a quest for tropical elements in architecture is now entangled with explorations of new modes of living within the realities of modern times in Indonesia.

Indonesia's numerous vernacular traditions have produced a range of strategies that have enabled generations of communities to endure the tropical climate and to live in harmony with the environment. The two key elements in the archipelago's vernacular architectural tradition are a living space raised above the ground, whether on a stone platform or a number of wooden stilts, and a dominant pitched roof. Raising the house above the ground not only creates a living space with a dry and well-ventilated floor but also provides protection from wild animals and insects, and the occasional flood. The pitched roof provides reliable protection from direct sunlight and downpours. Equipped with strategically placed ventilation outlets, this roof type also helps to create air circulation in the spaces below. The various ways in which the framework of the house is enclosed further ensure a constant flow of air. These environmental strategies were not only conceived as elements of architectural design but were part of the broader process of communal living and identity formation.

The formulation of tropical architecture outside the realm of the vernacular was first undertaken in Indonesia by Dutch architects working in the Netherlands East Indies, a colonial entity established in 1908 following more than three centuries of colonial expeditions throughout the vast archipelago now known as Indonesia.[9] During the 1920s, Dutch

Above From the outside, the A & M House in Kemang, Jakarta (page 72), resembles a modernist concrete, glass, and aluminum "container." In contrast, the interior embodies a more "open" environment—an open floor plan, expansive windows that let the outside in, natural materials, and a neutral palette—complemented by sleek modern furniture.

architects were confronted with a growing demand for government buildings, public facilities, and housing. They were also asked to create some kind of unified "Indies" architectural
identity in the midst of a racially, ethnically, and religiously segmented society. Two strands
of thought emerged. The first proposed that the cultivation of an indigenous Indies architecture should form the basis of an emerging "Indo-European" architectural style. The second
suggested that an "Indo-European" architectural style should be created as a tropical version
of the then Netherlands style since Indies indigenous architecture was seen as incapable of
addressing the requirements of modern living. Both parties, however, agreed on climatic
considerations in architectural design. Varying building types were subsequently produced.

Thomas Karsten and Maclaine Pont were proponents of the first concept. In their
buildings, for example the Sonobudoyo Museum in Yogyakarta and the People's Theater
in Semarang by Karsten and the Pohsarang Church and the ITB Main Hall by Pont, selected indigenous forms and climatic techniques were employed. Combined with these were
the use of modern construction methods and European concepts of formal architecture.
Reworking what was suggested as the peak of the Indies architectural tradition, Karsten
and Pont developed the Javanese *pendopo* pavilion typology as well as strategies of raised
space to fit new requirements and scales of buildings.[10] In residential architecture, indigenous

elements were combined to form the bungalow, a detached one-level structure. Each residential design was equipped with a semi-public verandah adjacent to a formal living room where guests were entertained. At the back of the house, a semi-open service corridor was created where native housemaids would perform their daily tasks. Thick brick walls enclosed the building and created an efficient temperature barrier, while hollowed cement blocks were installed at the lower and upper parts of the walls to ensure air circulation. All this contributed to an opening up of the European house typology to suit the tropical climate.[11] While 1930s Dutch-Indies architects did produce a range of sophisticated buildings, architectural historian Stephen Cairns has noted that they also perpetuated picturesque vernacular icons such as the *pendopo* as key design elements shaping modern architecture at the expense of more intangible elements relating to notions of community and use of space.[12]

Wolff Schoemaker, a proponent of the second strand of thought, produced a different type of tropical architecture, the most prominent examples being Vila Isola and the Preanger Hotel in Bandung, West Java. Given his doubts about the potential of Indies indigenous architecture to form the basis of an Indo-European architectural style, Schoemaker adopted European architectural elements, such as the concept of confined spaces and the geometry of the Art Deco style, and adapted them to the tropical climate by careful placement of openings in buildings and consideration of the transition between inside and out.

Following Indonesia's independence in 1945, new visions of the country's identity and the pursuit of "nation building" triggered a rethinking of Indonesian tropical architecture. In contrast to the promotion of indigenous building traditions during the colonial period, a modern architectural image, in particular the International Style, was strongly encouraged by the nation's first president, Sukarno. The objective was to demonstrate the capability of the newly independent state to adopt the modernity of developed countries.[13] Among the architectural landmarks of the Sukarno era are the National Mosque Istiqlal and the Bank of Indonesia headquarters, both in Jakarta, the capital. Designed by Indonesian planner and architect F. Silaban, these buildings adopted the International Style's geometric forms and concrete structural system.[14] In addition, site planning, landscaping, form and space were considered important strategies for dealing with local climatic conditions. In the Istiqlal Mosque, for example, the creation of distinctive building enclosures lowers the temperature and allows constant airflow through the building. A wall formed of precast hollow bricks arranged in a geometrical pattern encloses the complex and the inner prayer halls.

During the 1950s, Susilo came up with another interpretation of tropical architecture. In his design for the satellite town Kebayoran Baru in South Jakarta, built largely for civil servants and the capital's lower and middle classes, Susilo introduced a new building typology popularly called *jengki*, a term applied to a fashion trend at the time which was characterized by broad upper and narrow lower components. In Susilo's *jengki* house, a wide roof overhang shelters a narrower space below. Pentagonal-shaped walls enclose the two sides of the building, accentuating its unique proportions. Susilo also employed climatic devices once made popular by Dutch architects, such as the use of hollowed cement blocks and the creation of semi-open corridors and verandahs. Inside Susilo's *jengki* house, a variety of layouts were created in response to the economic status of buyers.

Left The Budi House (page 96) epitomizes architect Sardjono Sani's exploration of new construction methods, manufacturing techniques, and enlightened use of space in his effort to produce unique architectural compositions. Here, a sculptural staircase of laminated glass laid over a steel frame floats weightlessly to the second floor. "Cones" made of folded banana leaves topped with white flowers make a stunning arrangement on the slim cabinet sandwiched between the two flights of stairs.

These early experiments with modern Indonesian architecture were disrupted when Suharto came to power in the mid-1960s. His idea of Indonesian identity was to reintroduce the colonial version of a culturally rooted yet modern architecture. But unlike Karsten and Pont's creative borrowings of indigenous traditions, the interpretation of the vernacular during the New Order regime was largely one of superficial reproduction without adjustment to form or proportion, as can be observed in many government buildings. The desire for a modern architectural identity was also driven by the country's capitalistic economy. Extensive privatization of city infrastructures and housing projects left legacies such as corporate-style glass-and-steel structures. Residential designs were, and still are, dominated by pastiche reproductions of imagined "global" architectural styles such as Neo-Classical, European, American, and Mediterranean. Any insightful explorations of residential architecture by Indonesian architects were confined to the fringes of the country's housing industry.

At the end of the Suharto era, insecurity among Indonesia's upper middle and upper classes resulting from social turbulence caused by imbalances in the distribution of wealth and increasing displacement and marginalization of the poor, led not only to increasing polarization of Indonesian modern society but to an introversion of domestic living—a desire for houses where one could retreat and protect oneself from social and urban realities,

Above The Inke Gallery House in historic Menteng, Jakarta (page 176), is a handsome modern-day take on the traditional Chinese shophouse. The craftsmanship and the aesthetics of the terracotta and wood tones on the façade are carried through to the inside, where "unfinished" walls meet wood floors and hand-crafted objects in a fine display.

or from a deteriorating physical environment. Compounding the problem was the lack of large-scale housing initiatives and urban design agendas which mediate between *kampung-*style urbanity and its metropolis counterpart.[15] The face of modern housing and cities in Indonesia remains configured by stark social polarization and a fragmented urban environment. These are the broader contexts and challenges for the exploration of housing and tropical architecture in Indonesia. Yet, for the affluent minority, there will always be a demand for individual houses built on individual plots of land, although these locations will become increasingly expensive and removed from the main urban centers.

Contemporary Experiments in Tropical Housing in Indonesia

Today, many architects in Indonesia, albeit those involved in designing individual homes, are developing a new architectural consciousness. They are rejecting both the romanticized images of tropical architecture and the common reproductions of perceived tropical building solutions, capitalizing instead on the endless possibilities of architectural forms while selectively adopting elements of the country's architectural legacy. They are also focusing more on function, spatial arrangements, climatic considerations, and even affordability. The twenty-five houses discussed in this book thus offer explorations in architect-designed, climate-responsive, upper middle and upper class residential architecture in Indonesia.

In most of these modern homes, attempts are made to produce a more "open" environment. A gentle transition between the inside and out allows a constant channeling of air. Visual connectivity and physical interaction between spaces are sometimes alternated, at other times combined. Andra Matin's design for Permata Villa and Yori Antar's Dadit & Dina House are examples of this strategy. Notions of inside and outside are sometimes replaced by the creation of a continuous flow of space. The traditional courtyard house is also transformed through dynamic arrangement and the shaping of inner and outer spaces. Multiple courtyards and creative interlocking between building and landscape elements also occur. The designs of Tan Tjiang Ay's Prabowo House, Kusuma Agustianto's Setiadharma House, and Jeffrey Budiman's Suta House and Tantowi Residence demonstrate this trend.

Fresh ideas on the way in which people use their houses are also implemented. A house is no longer perceived as a series of enclosed rooms used for unrelated activities, but as a fluid interplay between private and public activities. In Andra Matin's design for Jane House and Yori Antar's Dadit & Dina House, semi-permanent, non-solid, and movable partitions are introduced as a way of separating spaces and zones of activity. Spatial fluidity is also explored in order to manipulate the sense of space within a narrow site or to offset the constraints of a building regulation. In the case of Adi Purnomo's Edi & Hetty Home, this is expressed through increasing the height of the ceiling and the floor platform beyond the interior, thus visually extending the sense of space beyond its actual dimensions.

A combination of landscaping and site leveling is explored in other projects to introduce new notions of the boundary between private houses and their surroundings. Through height differences and the placement of landscape elements, a spatial division is created without producing an abrupt divide. A sense of security is also achieved while avoiding massive fencing. This method can also lead to the creation of unique vertical circulation passages that can form both a corridor of light and a means of air circulation inside the house. Kusuma Agustianto's design for the Setiadharma House, Baskoro Tedjo's AB House, Andra Matin's Jane House, and Ahmad Djuhara's Tall House explore this strategy.

Creative ways of dealing with an urban site are revealed in Budiman Hendropurnomo's Howard House and Irianto PH's Amanda House. While Jakarta is now mostly known for its concrete jungle landscape, traffic jams, and introverted public spaces exemplified by the city's numerous shopping malls, these houses show us that one can live within, rather than avoid, the city. Selective framings of the surrounding scenery establish visual connections between a house and its setting. Baskoro Tedjo's AB House is a key example of this strategy, which in turn creates a rich spatial experience inside the house. A range of creative interpretations of colonial and vernacular architectural traditions are exemplified by the design of Yusman Siswandi's Inke Gallery House, Budiman Hendropurnomo's Howard House, Tan Tjiang Ay's appropriation of Chinese architectural typology in the Iskandar Residence, and Yori Antar's renovation of the Rino & Sarah Residence. Careful observation of the ordering of space and of proportion within certain vernacular and colonial architectural legacies have led to fresh interpretations, as have the use of different kinds of building materials. As an example, Ahmad Djuhara's Steel House, aside from its experimentation with recycled building materials, offers the reverse of the colonial domestic layout. The service area and staff quarters, traditionally hidden at the back of a house, are here situated at the front and, moreover, are treated as important elements of domestic living.

The twenty-five houses featured all illustrate, in one way or other, the dynamics of domestic living in contemporary Indonesia as aspired to by the country's upper middle and upper classes. A quest for tropical architecture takes place as an exploration of potentials of living in the tropics rather than as a search for one ultimate design formula or style. Explorations of new construction methods and manufacturing techniques and enlightened use of space are the key strategies from which these new architectural expressions emerge. With ready access to international architectural developments, contemporary Indonesian architects are increasingly familiar with, and sensitive to, current trends and aesthetics. Nonetheless, further experimentation with tropical architectural design in Indonesia is needed in order to find solutions to the pressing problems of urbanization and mass housing for the underprivileged majority: how to tackle urban growth and urban sprawl in an already dense tropical environment through new forms of housing; how to capitalize on local building conventions; how to give expression to housing in order to create a positive sense of neighborhood and urban culture; how to make architectural solutions accessible to a wide range of purchasing power. The most influential and exciting modern architecture projects worldwide are invariably the result of mediation with social and urban challenges. A discerning articulation of Indonesian tropical architecture can be further pursued through experimentations with new building programs and daring interpretations of new spatiality and building tectonics which address the country's potential and its challenges. For too long, the architecture of tropical Indonesia has been mistaken as a mere realm of exotic tropical houses and vernacular legacies, an architectural museum to which one may escape from Western urbanism and architectural modernity.[16]

Right The scale, layout, symmetry, and formality of the imposing Iskandar Residence (page 62) hark back to the architecture of Chinese Confucian temples and Dutch colonial mansions. Adapted here to suit a modern-day urban lifestyle, expansive glass windows and doors allow for views and access to the outside, while a wraparound terrace provides space for entertaining and dining.

Left At the back of the house, stilt-like supports, frameless glass walls, and pivoting wood panel doors contrast with the bold protruding box housing the master bathroom. All elements reflect the architect's interpretation of the modernist concepts of inside–outside, open–closed, and opacity–transparency.

Right A wild composition of interwoven rattan containing lighting forms an attractive screen between the living and dining areas backed by the pivoting doors that lead out to the garden, which is dominated by a single willow tree.

dadit & dina house

The design of the Dadit & Dina House originated from the clients' keen interest in modern architecture, especially the work of Ludwig Mies van der Rohe and Marcel Breuer. In terms of the spatial layout of their house, they asked architect Yori Antar to explore the modernist notions of inside–outside, open–closed, and opacity–transparency. The architect responded by designing a house with a distinct layering of spaces and an interplay of architectural elements. Two elements in particular—horizontal and vertical circulation—form a kind of translucent membrane that protects the main spaces of the house from the outside.

The dominant feature of the house and the innermost "sanctuary" is a dark box clad in *damar laut/bingkirai* wood (*Shorea glauca/Shorea laevis*) and coated with *lasur*, which extends from the balcony facing the street to the large bathroom window overlooking the back yard. The space beneath the box, which always remains "outside," forms a

PONDOK INDAH, JAKARTA

ARCHITECT YORI ANTAR
HAN AWAL & PARTNERS, ARCHITECTS

Above and opposite below Box-like showcases and a lit rattan screen separate the living and dining areas. Sofas and carpets designed by Melanie Hall of Mimpi Design lend a classical modern air to the living room. The pantry adjoining the dining area features a cement stove counter created by Yorgo Papadimitrou. The wooden dining table is by local designer Kamal.

Right The front elevation shows the use of machine-manufactured industrial products and hand-crafted natural materials: steel-framed polycarbonate sheets on the left, a timber-clad compart-ment supported on a steel frame on the right, and a pine log wall screen and glass walls below.

Opposite above The three levels of the house topped by a pitched roof screened by other elements.

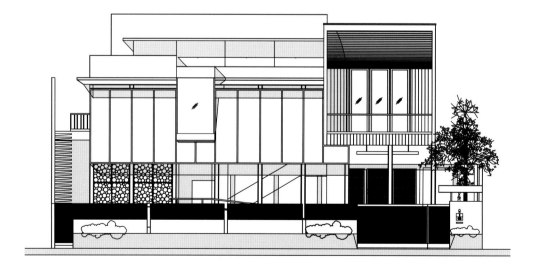

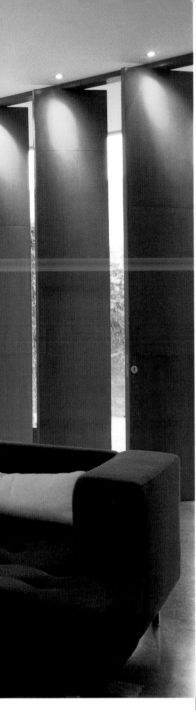

corridor that continues right through the building, allowing visitors to proceed directly to the garden at the back of the house or to enter the enclosed living room to the left of the corridor. The owners, who both work in the film industry, use the corridor space for viewing films and other functions. A reflecting pool alongside the corridor is a welcome cooling element.

The façade presents a combination of precise machine-manufactured industrial products and hand-crafted natural materials: a timber-clad compartment supported on a steel frame, transparent glass walls, movable polycarbonate louvers, a pine log screen wall. A ramp running along the verandah at the front of the house leads to the secondary or private entrance and to a staircase going to the upper stories. Similarly, the back of the house is an exercise in marrying man-made and industrial materials. The starkness of the building's glass and steel structure is balanced by the use of warm natural materials in the interior, and the use of highly textural linear plants along the perimeter wall.

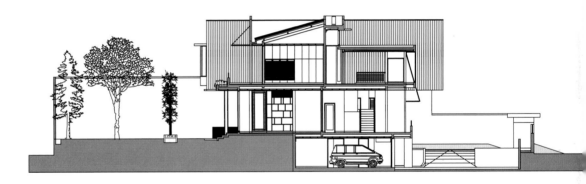

Opposite above The light and airy master suite, comprising bedroom, dressing room, and bathroom, stretches the entire length of the main timber-clad compartment. The curved ceiling in the bedroom relieves the rigidity of the "box."

Opposite below left In the children's bathroom, a white terrazzo sink and small white mosaic tiled walls offer a retro nuance.

Opposite below right A "transparent" staircase composed of painted checkered steel plates and steel wire leads to the bedrooms.

Right Flanked by a shower on the left and a toilet on the right, the big white terrazzo bathtub is placed in front of a large window overlooking the back garden. Glass projections above the terrazzo walls of the bath contain lighting.

Below A wall of sawn pine logs blocks views of the main entrance and aids air circulation. The crank allows movement of the polycarbonate louvers on the exterior.

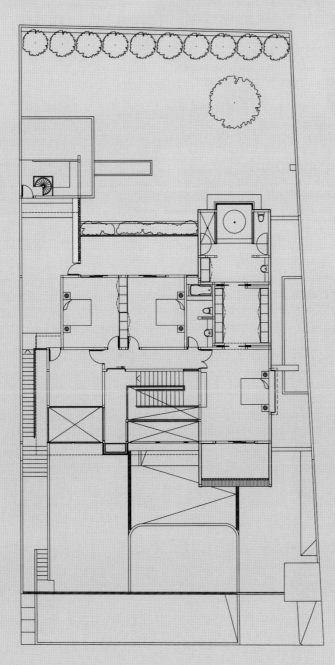

Opposite Pivoting doors and glass walls offer transparent views and access to the back garden. A band of gravel at the bottom of the terrazzo steps demarcates the house from the garden.

Above from left to right The timber-clad compartment facing the street does double duty as a drop-off canopy and balcony for the master bedroom.

The multifunctional corridor below the compartment is reached by steps, highlighted at night by concealed lighting, and a set of sliding glass doors. The garden is visible at the rear.

A ramp to the left of the public entrance leads to the private quarters of the house. The ramp is flanked by adjustable polycarbonate louvers and a transparent glass wall, both designed to mask views into the house from outside. The entrance to the house is to the right of the far wall composed of sawn pine logs painted black. A staircase inside the entrance leads to the bedrooms.

Left The upper (second) floor plan shows the dominant longitudinal box housing the master suite and the two children's rooms above the dining area. All bedrooms open on to a balcony at the back of the house, enclosed by planter boxes and iron balustrades. A spiral staircase gives access to the garden below.

suta house

Left From the street, the Suta House appears quite modest, with large regular openings placed on an inconspicuous façade. Vegetation concealing its tall, coarsely textured plaster perimeter wall is spotlighted at night. A sturdy gate made of glassfiber reinforced cement molded to look like stone forms a protective barrier.

Left From the street, the Suta House appears quite modest, with large regular openings placed on an inconspicuous façade. Vegetation concealing its tall, coarsely textured plaster perimeter wall is spotlighted at night. A sturdy gate made of glassfiber reinforced cement molded to look like stone forms a protective barrier.

Right The house centers around the main living room, an open space equipped with modern furniture and decorated with eclectic antique items and a baby grand.

PERMATA HIJAU, JAKARTA

ARCHITECTS JEFFREY BUDIMAN & JAMI HARWIG
J. BUDIMAN ARCHITECTS

The restrained elegance of the Suta House, located in the élite Permata Hijau district of South Jakarta, is in charming contrast to many of the other upscale homes in the area. While the majority of surrounding houses are defined by two-story-high façades supported by Corinthian or Ionic columns, or make stainless steel railings their main focus, the Suta House, situated on a modest 450-square meter plot, is composed of simple geometric masses. Pragmatic composition of spaces in the house and their efficient utilization make the house both comfortable and spacious.

Making the most of the small site, the architects opted to locate the main and most public area of the house on the first (ground) floor facing the road, with the service areas, comprising the garage, kitchen, laundry, and servants' quarters, in the basement below. The private spaces of the house, primarily the guest and family bedrooms, are arranged on an axis perpendicular to the main mass, on both the first and second floors.

Below and opposite above The living and dining areas occupy a single continuous space. A carved and painted work by Amrus Natalsya, set on a coarse textured wall at the end of the dining area, forms an eye-catching backdrop to the elegant modern furniture, antiques, and ethnic decorative items that fill the open-plan room.

A baby grand occupies a small extension off the living area. Wooden blinds along one side of the room moderate the light, while the dining area opens to an informal breakfast patio and the garden at the back of the house. Above the dining table, made of a solid piece of wood supported on a cubical base, an off-white fabric

stretched on a curved frame hides the lighting, at the same time forming a decorative element.

Bottom Section drawing of the house.

Opposite below A few well-chosen antique and ethnic objects make strong statements throughout the modern house.

The entrance to the house, accessed via a set of steps on the northeastern corner of the site, is located behind the main living space. Visitors entering the house do not directly intrude upon this space, but are diverted instead through a transitional corridor behind it, mimicking the function of the entrance foyer in traditional Indonesian homes. This corridor also allows the occupants of the house to come and go without disturbing the activities in the main living area. The arrangement thus maintains the clarity and purity of the living space, at the same time ensuring the privacy of its usage.

The main space, comprising an L-shaped open-plan dining area, sitting area, and adjoining music corner, wraps around a covered terrace with a table for casual dining. Beyond is the garden. This relatively public space directly faces the road but is shielded by full-length Venetian blinds on two sides. It is further protected from the outside by a row of thick piers that provides both a spatial and visual barrier as well as a perimeter wall. The dining area faces the road as well as the inner garden.

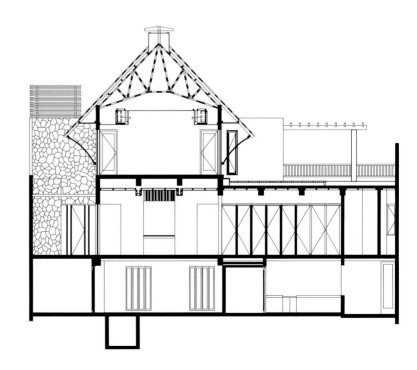

Above The symmetry of the
master bathroom, with its two
windows flanking a round mirror,
two wooden chests on either
side of a stand-alone *lavabo*, and
matching hanging lights, is coun-
terbalanced by the eclectic
mixture of ethnic and modern
elements.

Left and right Antique pieces
combined with newly designed
furniture that borrows from old
styles decorate the spacious
master bedroom. The modern
office chair, a contemporary
reproduction of the Aluminum
Group Executive Chair originally
designed in 1958 by Charles and
Ray Eames, is combined with a
super-realistic painting by Indonesian artist Rosid and old domestic objects to create a unique mix
in the room. Moderating the light,
Roman blinds give a veiled quality
to the room. The warm ambience
is enhanced by the wood parquet
flooring and throw rug.

Right In every corner of the master bedroom and bathroom on the second (upper) floor, sleek modern and warm natural or traditional elements are combined to give a domestic feel to an otherwise minimalist space. A large potted plant and a blooming orchid add a touch of green to the earthy tones.

Far right The green theme is carried over to the tinted glass wash basin and plant in the wood-panelled powder room on the first floor of the house.

On the second floor, directly above the living area, the master bedroom forms a perpendicular secondary mass that extends to the back of the site. The master bedroom opens out on three sides: to an entrance skylight on the left, to a roof deck and garden on the right, and, through connecting doors, to the children's bedrooms arranged behind the master bedroom on the same axis. The children's bedrooms are also accessed via an outer corridor. The master bathroom and a whirlpool adjoin the deck. The entire second floor can be sealed off from the rest of the house if necessary, during which time the doors of the rooms can be left open with confidence. Even if the outer corridor is not closed, the internal connecting doors can be left open to allow immediate access to all the rooms. Directly below the children's bedrooms, behind the main living area, are two guest bedrooms. In the same secondary mass, but in the basement below, is a music room and children's playroom.

The bedrooms on the first and second floors of the house look over a large garden on the southwest, which occupies about a quarter of the built-up area on the site.

The Suta Residence epitomizes architect Jeffrey Budiman's dictum of creating highly liveable spaces within a relatively modest enclosure, in which the experience of the house is to be enjoyed when spending time living inside. The clear composition and designation of spaces allows for the creation of a compact and comfortable environment.

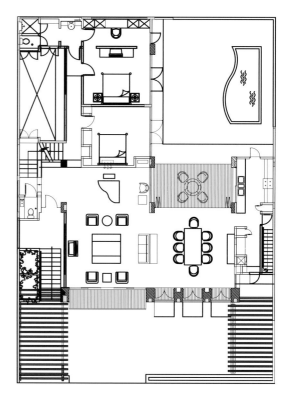

Above First (ground) floor plan.

Below The same granite flooring—smoothly shiny inside, matte on the outside—provides continuity and visually expands the space.

Right The enclosed wooden deck and grass-bordered pool off the master bedroom is the owners' favorite lounging space. It is a handsome solution in a house with a relatively small land area.

rino & sarah residence

Left Reflecting the owners' interest in cars and motorcycles, the residence has an aerodynamic quality about it. A play on opacity and transparency is apparent in its treatment of spaces, openings, and enclosures.

Right Mainly constructed of steel and glass and set on a concrete base, the transparent, cantilevered studio seems to float weightlessly over the pool. It acts as a kind of watch tower controlling every corner inside and outside the house.

PONDOK INDAH, JAKARTA

ARCHITECT YORI ANTAR
HAN AWAL & PARTNERS, ARCHITECTS

To design a house for a young couple with contrasting tastes challenged architect Yori Antar to come up with an architectural solution that, on the one hand, expressed their differences but, on the other, overcame them. Rino, the man of the house, is a great admirer of the simplicity and honesty of modern design, while his wife Sarah has a taste for the eclectic. The first floor—where Rino spends most of his time—is left transparent, while the second floor— where Sarah has more say—is encased in an opaque "skin."

From the street, the house appears as a box placed on stilts, reminiscent of Le Corbusier's Villa Savoie, and while it appears to be a two-story structure, the roof—which resembles the propped-up lid of a box—shelters another transparent story above, accommodating a gym. Hence, the four-story structure (including the basement housing

Above Texture, color, and strategically placed art characterize the interior of the house. In the living room, the minimalist architecture is filled with bold, modern furniture designed by Nada Daoudi Lahlou of Avant Garde Indonesia, who was called in to help Sarah combine her eclectic tastes with Rino's passion for modern styles. Black floor tiles define the living room space.

Left Originally designed strictly in black and white, the burnt orange furnishings and bamboo textures in Rino's study were later introduced to harmonize with the color scheme of the rest of the first floor and also to impart a masculine look—along with the black flooring. An elegant chaise longue and carved wood cabinets soften the workman-like interior.

Opposite Shattered glass panels sandwiched between sheets of plain glass overlook the stairwell, affording transparency as well as privacy and security.

Left A wood-framed glass counter for storing accessories makes an unusual centerpiece in the walk-in wardrobe-cum-dressing room sandwiched between the master bedroom and bathroom and set along the same axis. The bathroom forms a striking backdrop. Diffuse coffer lights above the dressing room, designed by Hadi Komara, mimic a skylight.

Below left The staircase leading to the bedrooms is lit by large windows facing the front of the house. At the bottom of the stairs, a decorative partition not only screens views from the road, but complements the modernist architectural look of the house. The railing is composed of laminated shattered glass set under a sturdy wood handrail.

Right In the master bathroom, a large travertine whirlpool bath is set on a "stage" flanked by two grand wood-encased columns and reached by wooden steps. The rust-colored travertine lining the middle part of the back wall forms a dramatic backdrop to the "stage," which is further enhanced by theatrical lighting.

Below right A blend of "his" and "her" styles occurs in the couple's bedroom. An eclectic mix of Mannerist furniture is set against intricately embossed wallpaper on one wall and a stylish combination of armoire and vitrine on another. The vaulted ceiling, waxed smoothly, and the lighting of the vitrine add to the richness of the décor.

a two-car garage, storage, driver's room, and security post), appears from the outside to be a simple two-story house.

Encased in glass, the entire first (ground) floor, for the most part, is visible from the street. Only a long balustrade of shattered glass placed in front of the stone-paved terrace and a fence of perforated steel running along the length of the site screen direct views into the house. There is an air of nonchalance about this house. Even the main dining room, which would be hidden in most conventional designs, is instead placed in front of the house, facing the street. A spacious pantry, complete with breakfast nook, leads to both living and dining rooms and to the poolside terrace behind. The kitchen, service areas, and maids' quarters wrap around the pantry. A view of the entire living room and entrance to the house is visible through the mirror glass walls of Rino's study, which projects out over the swimming pool on the far left corner of the site and the back garden. Throughout the first floor, the simplicity of the main building materials are offset by brilliant red accents in the furnishings.

On the second floor, reached by a matching crushed glass-bordered staircase inserted into the middle of the square box, lies the master bedroom suite, a self-contained longitudinal compartment running the entire right-hand side of the house. Another box adjoining it, almost square in plan, houses three bedrooms for the couple's children and a family room-cum-library. The encasement of the

second floor plays with the notion of opacity versus transparency on the façade of the house. It fragments the volumes and diverts the attention of the viewer away from the actual extent of the three-story volume of the house above ground.

A number of interior designers have been involved with this project: Hanky Tandayu developed the interior design for the master bedroom suite, Winda Siregar worked on the children's bedrooms, while elements in the common areas were created by Nada Daoudi Lahlou of Avant Garde. Various eclectic designs for the interior are set within the stark spaces of the first floor in such a way that the interior design and architecture complement each other.

Above At the back of the house, large wood-framed glass doors open to the tiled pool, its formal rectangular shape broken by the cantilevered study at the far end. Views of the roof garden above the study can be enjoyed from the back bedrooms and the third-story home gym.

Opposite above Laminated shattered glass is repeated in the railing bordering the verandah at the front of the house. Wooden doors at the end of the verandah lead directly to the dining room for more formal functions.

Opposite center Whimsical sculptures and other decorative art placed in strategic corners complement the strong lines of the building's architecture.

Opposite below The plans of the first floor (left) and second floor (right) show how the house is composed essentially of two volumes split by a central staircase. On the first floor, there is a distinct separation of living spaces (left) and service areas (right); on the second floor, the children's bedrooms and family room (left) abut the longitudinal master bedroom suite (right).

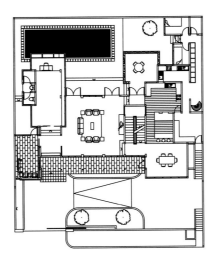

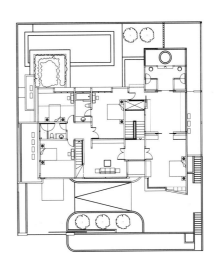

Above left Modern interpretations of classical Chinese furniture and a comical Ida Bagus Indra painting on a red background set the tone in the family room on the second floor—Sarah's space for her various activities. The staircase goes up to the third-floor gym.

Left A bright agra red wall greets visitors to the house, which is entered through a door encased within a wooden grill on the left. For formal functions, visitors can turn right up a ramp leading to the front verandah and enter the dining room at the far end.

Above Adjacent to the dining room, the pantry joins the drama of the interior décor. Designed by Ingrid Pranoto of Da Vinci, it is slick, fast, and modern with its bright Ferrari red finish and hi-tech appliances. A small dining island allows for quick breakfasts or casual dining.

prabowo house

Strict building regulations limiting the height of houses in this area to a single story, and the relatively spacious site, plus the laid-back nature of the owner couple, led accomplished architect Tan Tjiang Ay to make full use of the land area in order to create a "garden house." Throughout the long, narrow site, the built-up areas are arranged to complement open gardens, creating a balanced composition of positive and negative spaces.

The layout of the house also reflects Tan's questioning of established ways of thinking in Indonesian society. In this house, he discards the conservative and conventional progresssion of entrance, guest room, living room, and bedrooms common to most houses. Instead, he places the

KEMANG, JAKARTA

ARCHITECT TAN TJIANG AY

Above The heart of the house is the third of a series of volumes, located at the back of the house, which has direct access to a spacious open garden. The wide terrace becomes a transitional area between the outside and the inside, where the natural environment can be appreciated by relaxing on the large wooden divan. The concrete columns emphasize the simple modular geometry of the house. Entrance to the house is through large timber-framed doors, which add an overtone of warmth and intimacy to the house.

bedrooms at the front of the house so that visitors pass alongside them. Although the master bedroom has a full view of the gardens, the children's bedroom and study have limited views. These rooms are designed to reflect their primary function: private spaces in which to sleep or study, without distractions from outside.

The volumes are designed as gable-roofed boxes, open in plan. The simplicity of the spaces within is compensated by the complexity of the arrangement of spaces. Hierarchy is not created by the enlargement of elements, but rather by the way they are put together. The house is entered through a simple metal grill door sandwiched between two gable-roofed structures. In line with Tan's thinking, these accommodate very different functions, ones that are not usually placed together. The one on the left houses a double garage, while the one on the right accommodates the children's bedrooms and study. The two structures are separated by a shallow reflecting pool.

Alongside the garage is a narrow corridor leading to the center of the site and a third gable-roofed structure. This third volume, also open in plan but bordered by a covered patio along its full length, houses the living and dining areas, the heart of the house.

Also facing the vast open garden is the master bedroom on the north end of the first volume. This volume is divided into three main rooms, with bathrooms in between. Adjacent to the master bedroom is a children's bedroom, while a study is placed in the south end to the front of the house. The study has no openings to the front of the house. The openings of the three rooms are all arranged on the north wall, with the exception of the master bedroom which also takes advantage of the view to the open space to the north.

While the service areas of the house, including the laundry, storage, and servants' quarters are arranged along the wall on the far left (north) of the site, the kitchen is strategically placed in the center of the site, functioning as a kind of pivot that links the three main volumes of the house together.

Left The living and dining areas are contained in a single space. The simplicity of the house's geometry is echoed in the minimalist furniture and the unfussy materials used for the walls, doors, and floors.

Above The living and dining area extends out to a small patio at the back of the house. The axial character of the design is emphasized by the corresponding doors and the flanking chairs. A door at the far end of the living and dining room leads to the kitchen.

Right A different view of the living and dining room shows the relatively long, narrow space. The woven-backed dining chairs harmonize with the wooden latticework living room and patio chairs.

Left The modest façade of the house reflects its internal architectural composition. The transparent entrance is flanked by two gable-roofed volumes. The gable to the left is spare, suggesting the functionality of the garage housed within its volume. In contrast, the gable to the right is crowned with a terracotta tile roof, suggesting the more domestic nature of the rooms within.

Below left and right Sharing space with the garden at the back of the house, the third-volume living room is also crowned with a terracotta tile roof, again suggesting a domestic space. The flat-roofed verandah, supported by concrete pillars, extends the full length of the living area, forming a natural transition between the building and its surroundings.

Right The floor plan of the single-story house reveals the juxtaposition of built-up areas, paths, and gardens.

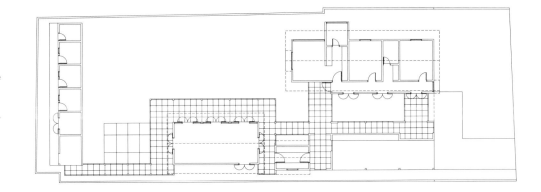

Left A stone finial from Central Java takes pride of place on a pedestal in the middle of the inner courtyard. The courtyard is designed in strict symmetry. Behind the stone ornament is a false façade that mirrors the rear elevation of the house facing the courtyard. Flanking the courtyard, the glass-encased modern "boxes" also mirror one another.

Right The living room on the first (ground) floor faces the courtyard. Framing the view are three tall, timber-cased glass doors inspired by doors in colonial houses in Indonesia. The simple pattern of the polished cement floor reflects the geometry of the architecture.

solo home

KEBAYORAN BARU, JAKARTA

DESIGNER JAYA IBRAHIM
JAYA & ASSOCIATES

In response to the commercialization of some of the areas surrounding the residential district of Kebayoran Baru, and the accompanying changes in traffic patterns, the owners of this home decided to build a townhouse that could also be used to showcase classic Indonesian furniture, fittings, and artifacts in the type of home setting for which the products were originally made.

Designer Jaya Ibrahim, whose passion is preserving the style of residential architecture of Java's big cities towards the end of the colonial period, seized the opportunity in the Solo Home to combine the colonial and the contemporary, blending elements from colonial Indonesian architecture with the cleaner and simpler minimalist style of today. Similarly, materials that have been used in Indonesian houses since colonial times are here incorporated in more modern designs and construction. The result is a house containing the designer's personal mixture of architectural and cultural elements, old and new, from East and West.

The architectural composition of the house comprises four boxes sheltered within the canopy of a hip roof. The box in front is a single-story volume resembling a light-colored monolith, projecting out towards the front of the site. It encloses the foyer of the house in lieu of the veran-dah which was characteristic of houses in the 1930s and 1940s. The main volume of the house occupies the second, central box, which stretches the entire width of the site. The third and fourth boxes are placed on either side of the central box, at the back of the site, flanking an open court-yard which is the focal point of the house.

Below and opposite above The side walls of the spacious family room on the second floor are filled with bold, symmetrical white shelving, specially designed for displaying elegant objects. The composition is broken by fabric-covered panels. A wooden grill below the ceiling acts as a kind of cornice while also hiding the air-conditioning units. An intricate basket-weave latticed screen in front of the doors lead-ing to the balcony modulates both views and light. The terrazo floor-ing reflects the geometry of the

architecture. Large comfortable sofas, brightened with colorful scatter cushions, complement the room's strong lines.

Below right Entry to the master bedroom is through a narrow passage culminating in a modern-ist wooden pedestal bearing a wooden bowl. This passage, which becomes an anteroom for ensur-ing privacy, leads to the master bedroom on the left and the dressing room/walk-in closet and bathroom on the right.

The spacious foyer dominating the front volume greets visitors to the house. As they enter, the sounds of water can be heard trickling down the horizontal strips of granite that line both walls, the projections and crevasses in the strips creating a syncopated rhythm in the waterfall. The water flows down to a linear pool that literally delineates the area of the foyer, creating a threshold between the foyer and the main showcase-cum-living space.

The living room is filled with elegant furniture and decorative items appropriate for a living and dining room. To one side of the living room is a show bedroom while the opposite side is occupied by a show sitting room.

The entire first level of the house is covered with a tinted polished cement floor. Although inspired by the flooring fashion of the 1930s–40s fashion in which small factory-produced tinted cement floor tiles were used, here the cement is poured in situ, resulting in a harmonious blend with the glossy new elements which have been incorporated into the house using inexpensive old materials.

Tall tripartite doors, derived from 1940s colonial architecture, mark the end of the living space. While colonial-period doors were usually painted, here the jambs have been stripped bare of paint or ornamentation, the frames have been subtly painted a grayish hue, and the panels have been replaced with glass—in line with the architect's more modern treatment of the first, third, and fourth "boxes."

Beyond the living space is the main focal point of the house—the courtyard—which is enclosed by the second, third, and forth volumes and the back wall of the house. A Central Javanese stone finial, presumed to have adorned a prominent town wall around the sixteenth or seventeenth century, is set on a cemented brick pedestal, which also serves as a fountain, in the middle of a shallow, stone-lined reflective pool bordered by a bed of river stones. Behind the ornament is a false façade, introduced to provide symmetry to the spatial composition. To the left and right of the courtyard are the modern volumes, encased in glass with aluminum frames, and painted a dark brown. Their façades mirror each other, further contributing to the spatial symmetry of the courtyard. These spaces house the kitchen and pantry on the left and an informal dining/family room and study/office on the right.

The second floor of the house is dominated by the family sitting room, which extends from the balcony above the foyer in front right to the back where it overlooks the courtyard. The master bedroom, with attached dressing area/walk-in closet and bathroom, occupies the wing to the right, overlooking the courtyard, and is entered through a narrow passageway from the living room. On the other side of the family room, directly opposite the master bedroom, is a smaller study and bathroom. Access to the second floor is via a stairway leading off the courtyard.

Left A set of Water Spies water-colors of grasshoppers, painted in Bali in the 1920s, and a pair of tall wood-framed glass doors form a backdrop to the sitting room on the first floor. In front of the doors are two contemporary in-terpretations of Khmer-shaped bowls placed on cement pedestals.

Right The plans of the first floor (left) and second floor (right) show clearly the symmetrical arrange-ment of the "boxes," culminating in the enclosed courtyard at the back of the house.

Below The backdrop of the show bedroom mirrors that of the sitting room on the opposite side of the ground floor, but the Spies watercolors are replaced here with a large mirror. The red, white, and blue color scheme, inspired by royal colors of the colonial past, provide a fresh contrast to the earthen tones of the furniture and architectural elements.

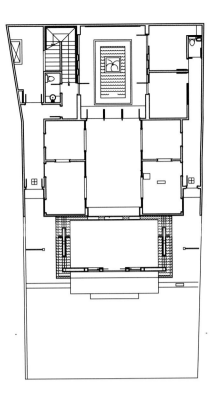

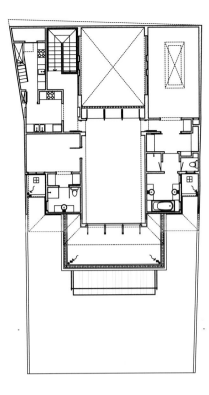

Above left An unusual feature of the master bedroom—again harking back to colonial architecture—is the raised ceiling whose row of clerestory openings bring natural light into the room. Behind the bed, prints of Neo-Classical architecture are set on a panel covered with Javanese *lurik* fabric. The furnishing fabrics used throughout the house, supplied by Wieneke de Groot/Nilamare, are made from vegetable dyes and were hand-spun, hand-loomed, and hand-woven in Tuban, East Java. The parquet flooring and cream carpet add to the cosy feel of the bedroom.

Left The arrangement of the furniture in the study opposite the master bedroom reflects the simple, symmetrical composition of the home's architecture. The door into the study is covered with fabric from Tuban. All the furniture in the house was designed by Jaya Ibrahim, whose inimitable flair and attention to detail are apparent in every room.

Above and right Terrazzo is the dominant material used in the bathroom: the room is lined in terrazzo; the floor is covered with terrazzo strips in contrasting cream and gray colors, inspired by the stripes in Javanese *lurik* fabric; the bathtub placed at the end of the room is set on a low terrazzo base; and on either side of the room are twin terrazzo-lined basins set in identical cabinets. A toilet in the alcove on the left and a shower on the right complete the bathroom suite. More prints of Neo-Classical architecture add interest above the tub. The view of the bathroom from the master bedroom shows the transition in the flooring, from soft, warm, earthen-toned dark wood to hard, cold, bright-colored terrazzo. A pair of latticed sliding doors offer privacy in the dressing area and bathroom.

iskandar residence

KUNINGAN, JAKARTA

ARCHITECT TAN TJIANG AY

In designing this house for an established couple with independent, grown-up children, architect Tan Tjiang Ay took into account the relatively small 800-square meter site at his disposal as well as the formal nature of the owners. Set in an élite neighborhood not far from the center of Jakarta, the mansion Tan designed is reminiscent, in both scale and layout, of classical Chinese architecture, particularly the architecture of Confucian temples, as well as the tropical landhouse mansions that the Dutch built on the outskirts of Jakarta in the eighteenth and nineteenth centuries. Here, Tan has reinterpreted these early forms to suit a modern-day urban lifestyle.

The main mass of the house, situated at the very heart of the site, is a two-story structure sheltered by a large hip roof, supported by rectangular columns, which extends over the terraces surrounding the house. Behind the main volume is a secondary mass that houses various supporting rooms. To the left of the main structure is a garage and servants' quarters, while the length of the right side of the site is occupied by a long lap pool.

Left The living room runs across the width of the house on the ground floor, one end occupied by seating, the other by a grand piano. Expansive glass windows and doors on three sides allow for a sweeping view of the surrounding gardens as well as access to the verandah and to casual sitting and dining areas on the terrace, one adjacent to the lap pool. During the heat of the day, the verandah filters heat and light entering the house and also protects the occupants from views from the street. At night, translucent blinds roll down to mask the space. The simple off-white, orange-red, gray, and black color scheme and the use of painted plaster and wood are carried throughout the house.

Visitors enter the imposing structure via a flight of steps which lead to the main living room, complete with baby grand, surrounded by mirror glass walls and sliding doors to the terraces. The starkness of the façade is softened by potted plants, trees and bushes, and grass set in hollowed tiles in an intricate geometric pattern.

Above the spacious living room is the master bedroom suite, a modest space reached by a striking yellow spiral staircase, with an adjoining bathroom and walk-in closet. A study occupies the opposite end, while a bridgeway leads from the bedroom suite to the secondary structure behind.

The secondary mass, also two stories in height, houses a state-of-the art kitchen on the left, with a music room above it, and two guest rooms with ensuites, stacked one above the other, at the opposite end. Sandwiched in between is the formal dining room that extends two stories high through a void. Above the music room is a third story tucked under the roof, which is used for aerobics and other fitness activities.

All the bedrooms are placed adjacent to the lap pool, contributing to the more relaxed character at the back of the house. A table for informal dining adjacent to the pool adds to the casual atmosphere.

Left From the outside of the house, the height of the verandah ceiling gives the impression of a vast space. In reality, the tiled verandah is a rather narrow area between the inside and outside. More than anything, it functions as a transition zone or "filter" into the house.

Above Although rather narrow, the double-height dining room located in the center of the secondary volume has an air of grandeur. Two wood carvings add to the verticality. The red silk runner dressing the eight-seater dining table, the off-white upholstery, shiny black tiles, wood, glass, and plaster continue the decorative theme.

iskandar residence 67

Above The master suite above the living room in the main mass of the house—reached by a yellow spiral staircase—comprises a study at one end, the bedroom in the middle, and a walk-in closet at the other end, all unified by continuous wood flooring. Adjacent to the bedroom and closet is a granite-lined bathroom. A painting by Hanafi above the bed complements the warm tones of the furnishings and wood-lined window.

Left The spiral staircase connecting the levels of the main volume is one of the few curved elements in the house. It softens the appearance of the otherwise strictly formal architectural composition.

Right The futuristic Norman Foster desk in the study dominates the space and stands in stark contast to the yellow painted walls and warm wooden floor. Broad windows on two sides let in light and air.

Right The black granite walls of the bathroom and bathtub base form a stark backdrop to the pristine white bathtub, glass shower cubicle, and shelving units. A slit window lets in natural light. Candles and orchids add ambience.

Below A state-of-the-art kitchen located on the ground floor at one end of the secondary volume is decorated in a two-tone color scheme composed of reddish-brown wood and stark black granite. The staff quarters are conveniently located off one end of the kitchen and the dining room the other.

Below left and right Classical formality typifies the first (left) and second (right) level floor plans. The main mass placed at the heart of the site is connected to the secondary mass behind by a terrace on the first floor and by a bridgeway on the second. The lap pool on the right runs the length of both structures.

Bottom Laden with *fengshui* overtones, a large dark-lacquered wooden screen at the back of the living room acts as a modern-day "spirit wall," shielding direct views into the dining area in the secondary structure beyond and ensuring a favorable flow of energy.

Opposite Despite its simple, open plan, modern materials, and clean, sleek lines, each area of the house has its unique character. The outdoor dining area, placed simply at the end of the longitudinal main space, next to the lap pool, offers a more relaxed environment for the owners and their guests.

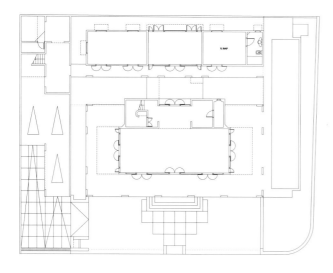

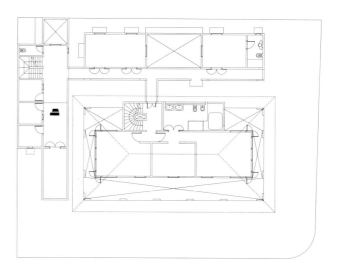

a & m house

KEMANG, JAKARTA

DESIGNER TED SULISTO
TED SULISTO DESIGN ASSOCIATES

Although many examples of contemporary architecture have sprouted up all over Jakarta, the appearance of a stark gray box in the middle of a modest upper middle-class neighborhood at the periphery of the élite residential district of Kemang, South Jakarta, continues to bewilder neighbors and passers-by. While the spareness of its form startles viewers, it is the scale and proportion that mostly baffle them. The severe gray box, formed of solid planes of concrete pierced by a full-height entrance and long, narrow windows, its starkness relieved to some extent by an aluminum and glass overhang, appears small. It is, in fact, a two-level structure poised above a third level: a basement partially submerged on the left beneath the sloping site but at full-story height on the right. A swimming pool runs along the whole left side of the house at the level of the first (ground) floor, while a skylit staircase located in the center of the house and a further lightwell in the far right corner open up this modernist "container."

Left A warm, sunny palette infuses the interior of the house. Here, in the entrance, visitors are greeted by an earth-toned upholstered bench, a brilliantly hued abstract painting, and wood paneling and flooring. The frosted glass screen masks the staircase behind it.

Below and right In the gray-walled audio-visual corner of the open-plan living room, located between the black-walled study at the front of the house and a small garden at the rear, a large white sofa and two Mies van der Rohe Barcelona chairs covered in ochre-colored leather face the large flat-screen television and audio equipment. Another sitting area faces the swimming pool.

Overleaf Translucent glass, stainless steel finishes for door and window frames and furniture, black leather upholstery, painted plaster walls, a white ceiling, and parquet flooring contribute to a Zen mood in the living/dining area. The graceful curve of a standing lamp offsets the strong lines.

Visitors enter the house via a set of stairs ascending a massive, granite-clad projection bordered by a clear glass railing and topped by a canopy. The porthole-type window in one end of the projection allows views inro a small room in the basement.

Beyond the small foyer at the entrance and the staircase leading to the upper level of the house is a large, open, L-shaped space housing, first, the living room which runs across the width of the ground floor and, beyond it, on the long end of the "L," the dining area and adjoining kitchen demarcated by a breakfast bar. One side of the living area and the dining area face the swimming pool through full-length stainless steel-framed glass doors. A steel and glass canopy shields the inside from rain. A wood-planked deck surrounds the pool, which is also shielded from view by a block wall clad in slate and a frosted glass partition above. A matching wall at the end of the pool hides the wet kitchen extension and blocks views of the site behind. On the right front of the house, a study leads off the living area. In the far right corner, a planted lightwell fills the house with color, air, and light.

The skylit staircase in the middle of the first floor not only demarcates the division between public and private spaces but also leads to the second floor where all the bedrooms are located. The master bedroom, together with its bathroom and walk-in closet, is arranged longitudinally above the living and dining areas and kitchen on the first floor. Two of the children's bedrooms face the front of the house, above the entrance, while a third bedroom faces the lightwell in the far right corner. The first bedroom has an adjoining bathroom while the other two share one.

The service areas of the house—the staff quarters, including a kitchen, the laundry, and storage—are placed in the basement level, along with a multi-car garage running from the front of the house to the skywell at the back. A music room is sandwiched in the middle, adjoining the garage. From this room, the inside of the swimming pool can be seen through porthole-type openings.

In contrast to the modernist exterior of the house, the gleaming interiors are imbued with a feeling of lightness and openness, the result of a combination of a simple open-floor arrangement, expansive picture windows that open to the pool, and the judicious use of skylights. The décor—colorful and eclectic—is infused with the many creative ideas of designer Ted Sulisto. Only the best available products and materials have been used. The rather simple structural "enclosure" is thus a perfect showcase for the spaces it contains.

Left and above Lit from below, the translucent glow of the laminated frosted glass floor leading from the foyer to the living/dining room forms a brilliant contrast to the opacity of the wood floor in the living area, the dark wood veneer on the staircase, and the black furnishings. The frosted glass walls of the foyer curtain off the pool and living spaces, yet allow ample light to enter.

Right The music room in the basement is a cozy private lounge with a large, comfortable, off-white sofa, where the owners of the house can enjoy listening to music, watching movies, or simply relaxing. The interior of the swimming pool can be viewed through three circular portholes cut into the wall behind the sofa.

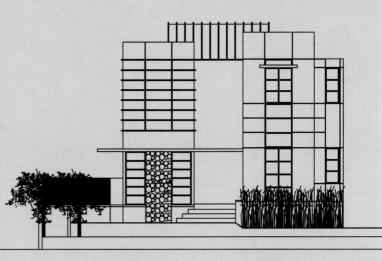

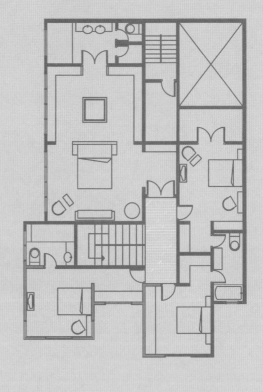

Above left Wood flooring, unusual in a bathroom, contrasts beautifully with the marble, glass, and stainless steel in the master bathroom. A pair of glass bowl wash-basins mounted on a marble-top wood cabinet are flanked by a long bath on one side and glass-encased toilet and shower cubicles on the other.

Left Bomba bar stools meet brushed steel in this high-tech kitchen located at the end of the dining area. An island indented with a sink and cooker, under a suspended hood, becomes a table for informal dining. The cabinets and appliances built into the far wall add to the uncluttered look.

Above The front elevation of the stark gray box (above), and the second-floor plan (below) showing the three smaller bedrooms wrapped around the master suite.

Above and below right The focal point of the bedroom is the large liquid crystal display screen television mounted on a black cabinet. Recessed ceiling lighting adds a soft glow to the room. A spacious dressing room separates the bedroom and bathroom, its tall frosted-glass door cabinets providing plenty of storage. A large divan fills the middle of the space. Continuous parquet flooring unifies the bedroom suite.

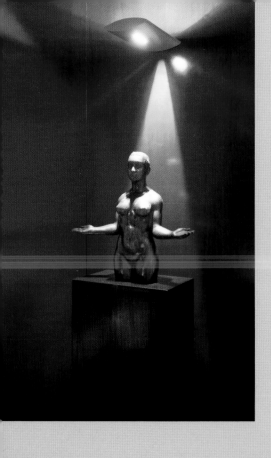

Opposite from left to right Steel-framed glass forms a striking modernist canopy at the entrance to the house. Horizontal wood slats on the façade above provide a contrast in color and texture.

A steel-framed skylight hovers over the staircase in the center of the house, bringing in light and breaking up the spaces.

In the guest bathroom on the ground floor, a glass bowl wash-basin and mirror-covered cabinet are mounted on the wall, freeing the small area from the need for a counter.

A theatrically lit statue on a podium under the central stair-case adds color and drama.

Left Another view of the swimming pool showing the living room to the left. Frosted-glass panels are mounted above the simple brick wall clad with slate, further mask-ing views into the pool area.

Right By night, the artfully lit façade of the house plays a differ-ent tune. Lighting set into the granite podium and spotlights highlighting the walls and canopy produce a theatrical effect.

Left A large, sparkling pool lies at the heart of the family compound, and it is here that the occupants of three houses gather to swim and socialize. Visually framed by the bridge connecting the house to the parent's home, the pool is surrounded by lawns dotted with palms and other tropical foliage.

Right A canopy of thin concrete supported by an inverted L-shaped concrete structure and a concrete frame box clad with horizontal wood slats mark the entrance to the house. From the box, visitors walk down an open plaza that leads to the actual entrance.

permata villa

PERMATA HIJAU, JAKARTA

ARCHITECT ANDRA MATIN
ANDRA MATIN ARCHITECT

Located in a large family compound in the middle of Jakarta, this house is one of three on the site. The owner's parents live in an adjacent house, which is attached to the third house occupied by his sibling. The three houses are grouped towards the front of the compound, allowing for a vast, common, open space at the back, the focus of which is a large swimming pool.

The overall plan of the house includes three distinct masses superimposed on each other, with the central mass tying the others together. From the street, the house appears somewhat uninviting, fortified as it is by a modulated wall with small fenestrations. The entrance, which is skewed at an angle of forty-five degrees, is reached by tiled steps, which lead into a cube screened by narrow bands of wood. The house proper is entered at the far end of the cube.

Right The living room takes full advantage of the large site and high elevation on which the house stands, commanding views of the garden and swimming pool through large timber-framed glass doors along three sides of the room. Thin wooden blinds screen views and light. The zebra striped carpet is a humorous touch and offsets the formality of the room.

Below A set of steps leads to the living room, raised considerably higher than the garden. Pivoted on floor hinges, the timber-framed glass doors allow the spaces to flow seamlessly into one another.

Opposite below The front (left) and back (right) elevations show the cube-like formality of the architecture and the complex composition of elements.

Harmonizing with the slats on the cube are wooden "grilles" screening the windows on the first and second floors. A tall white wall with a single elongated window on the third floor forms the front of the house. Once inside, the architect has modulated the volumes and planes and offered further spatial variety by playing with the heights of the spaces and the shapes of the openings.

The main, central mass accommodates a formal dining room in the middle of the first floor that extends to an airy, open living room at the rear. Continuous black granite flooring throughout the living and dining areas allows the spaces to flow seamlessly into one another. A spiral staircase in the corner of the living room leads down to a games room. Above, on the second floor of the central mass—reached by a centrally located staircase—is a central family room extending back to the master bedroom.

The second and third masses are pulled out towards the front of the house, creating a kind of open plaza that

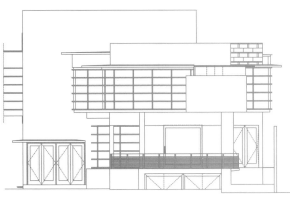

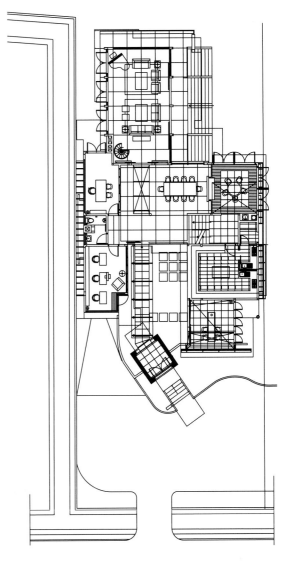

Left The front entrance expresses the play of planes and volumes found throughout the house. The wide horizontal strips of wood covering the windows help shade the interiors from direct sunlight while bringing in reflected light.

Below The first floor plan shows the formal dining room and living room in the central mass, the two studies in the second mass on the left, and the informal dining area, kitchen, and reception room in the third mass on the right.

Left Yellow and white chairs add to the casual air of the double-height informal dining space. The corridor above leads to the bridge connecting the parents' place.

Below left A section view through the house, from the front entrance on the left to the back of the house on the right.

Below A sculpture on a lightbox adds a dramatic note to this otherwise honey-colored formal dining room. Beyond the low wall at the end is the casual dining area. Black granite flooring reinforces the sense of space on the first floor.

leads to the entrance. The second mass, on the left of the entrance, contains a study for the master of the house on the first floor and another study for the children. Above, on the second floor, are two children's bedrooms.

The third mass, to the right of the central structure, contains the kitchen, a casual dining room, and a room where drop-in visitors can be received without inviting them into the house proper. Above, on the second floor, a larger children's study-cum-games room projects out, opening to the entrance plaza. Another room is placed on the interior mezzanine level of the study.

In contrast to the protective screens at the front of the house, large openings characterize the back, allowing the garden and pool to be seen from the master bedroom as well as the living and dining areas of the house.

Although designed as a self-contained unit, the house is connected to the others in the compound via a bridgeway at the second level. This allows the parents of the owner to visit their grandchildren and vice versa without having to go up and down any stairs or in and out of the entrances. The structures of the houses, crowned by the bridgeway, create an entrance gateway to the vast open space around the swimming pool, the area most commonly shared by all the occupants of the compound.

Above A corner off the living room on the second level, raised on a wooden platform, commands views of the garden and swimming pool.

Left A bright red reading chair is a bold presence in a corner of the master study on the first floor. The door leads to the gangway which runs along the perimeter wall on the left of the site.

Right The second floor plan shows the location of the family room and master bedroom in the central mass, two bedrooms flanking adjoining bathrooms in the second mass on the left, and a games room in the right-hand mass, with a third bedroom on the interior mezzanine level above it.

Opposite The third children's bedroom, on the interior mezzanine level of the games room, is covered with warm wood flooring, which complements the sturdy wooden treads of the staircase springing from the floor of the games room.

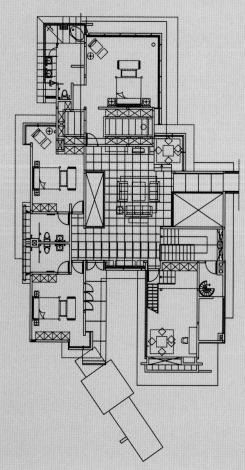

Opposite Two rows of illuminated paving stones set at right angles in a pond in the entrance plaza lead to the living room on the left and to the reception room for drop-in visitors on the right. The far corner of the pond is illuminated by a series of box lights which act as a skylight for the basement garage.

Left Another view of the entrance structure, slanted at a forty-five degree angle, which greets visitors to the house.

Below Near the pool, a wooden screen blocks views of the outdoor shower, washbasin, and changing room. The changing room is essentially a concrete niche equipped with swinging wooden doors on steel poles.

Left A suspended dark wood and glass entrance canopy, a dramatic curved metal roof, a variety of perforations in the white concrete façade, and black andesite stone lining the base of the house combine to create a rhythmic composition of light and dark.

Right A sculptural staircase of laminated glass on a steel frame, its treads lit up at night, appears to float weightlessly on its way to the second floor. A simple cabinet in the narrow sliver between the lower and upper part of the stairs is an ideal showcase for treasures.

budi house

The sudden presence of a stunning composition of pristine forms on the Wungkal Hill surprises passers-by as well as the residents of Semarang, Central Java, which lies to the east, much like the revelations of the latest make of car at an automobile show. The three-story residence of automobile dealer Budi Taruno and his wife Lilly has been deliberately designed to reflect the owners' obsession with the automobile: the sophistication of its engine and the elegance and aesthetics of its streamlined aerodynamic forms. The main components of the house, built of concrete, corrugated metal, and glass, are detached architectural elements that have seemingly been derived from the automobile engine.

Architect Sardjono Sani believes that every architectural creation is a unique response to a number of factors. Every site, client, program, and social and cultural context differ and, hence, the architectural outcome is truly unique. Above all, Sardjono avoids developing a particular "style" in his works, and this house, one of his most recent creations, is evidence of this philosophy.

WUNGKAL, SEMARANG

ARCHITECT SARDJONO SANI
BIAS TEKNO-ART KREASINDO

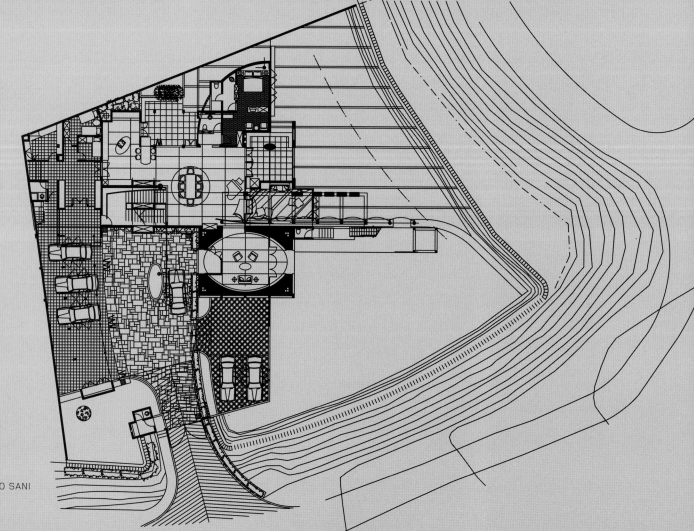

Above left Laminated glass laid over a water reservoir and lit with blue tube lights forms a highly original floor in the sunken sitting area. The blue glow and reflections from the movement of water below add a sensual touch. A row of round plastered concrete columns, painted gray, extends from the sitting room to an open patio.

Right The sitting room is entered from inside the house through a pair of tall wood-framed doors flanked by low soapstone pedestals from Yogyakarta. Its laminated glass flooring is in stark contrast to the white marble used in the living room on the right. Black granite borders the space, enhancing the oval shape of the living room.

Below left The first floor plan shows the orientation of the main elements towards the east.

Below A bed of white gravel leading to doors on the opposite side of the sitting room adjoins the patio paved in andesite stone.

Left The laminated glass staircase ends at a bridge that leads to the oval family room on the second floor. The ceiling above the staircase is lined with a subtly colored sycamore veneer. A narrow skylight adds more light to an already bright and airy house.

Above A combination of wood and glass is used for the flooring at the entrance to the marble-floored oval family room, located directly above the oval living room. The tall glass walls offer panoramic views of the surroundings. Sycamore veneer covers the ceiling.

Below As this east elevation shows, rectangular elements of various dimensions at the center of the composition, punctuated by expansive windows and a pool on the second floor, point towards a view of Semarang city to the east.

Left The oval area on the ground floor, designated the living room, is in fact quite open and can also be used for other functions. The centerpiece, a large, formal flower arrangement on a podium, sits surrounded by views of the garden. Visible through the glass walls is the outdoor staircase leading to the pool on the second floor.

Below and above right A large, lofty area just inside the entrance extends two stories high through a circular void in the middle. Leading off it are the living and sitting rooms on the right (east) and the staircase to the upper levels on the left (west). The space can also be used as a formal dining room.

Below right A small inner terrace offers a space for more relaxed, less formal dining. While it gives the impression that it is located outside the house, it is placed inside, though its sides are open. Fine bamboo softens the high perimeter wall. A bright hanging lamp adds a colorful touch to the pale walls and flooring.

None of the elements in the architectural composition conforms to the irregular geometry of the site. Rather, the strong central axis, oriented towards views of Semarang, is the main factor determining the layout of the house. The strong axis is reinforced by rectangular elements of various sizes at the center of the composition, all "pointing" east, ending with an azure pool on the second story.

Above the entrance, an extraordinary vertical plane of corrugated metal, supported by a simple concrete frame, extends upwards and then curves towards the east. This seemingly aerodynamic roof not only becomes a symbol of the owners' keen interest in cars, but also channels morning light into the house and blocks afternoon sun.

The living room, located just inside the entrance, is oval in plan, yet enclosed within a rectilinear frame, echoing the rectangular plan on the other side of the central axis. Leading off the living room is a formal dining area and, beyond that, the kitchen with attached breakfast bar, and other service areas. A guest suite to the right of the kitchen opens up to a patio, which is also accessible from the main entrance and the living room.

Echoing the plan of the first floor, an oval-shaped, glass-lined family room and the master bedroom on the first floor face east towards Semarang, the infinity pool sandwiched between them. Likewise, a studio-office on the third floor faces east. The rest of the second floor is occupied by three bedrooms on the west side.

Left Shards of light dance on the day bed in the sitting area adjoining the master bedroom courtesy of the skylight above. The lime green of the cushions picks up the colors in the painting by Srihadi.

Right The spacious master bedroom suite on the second floor of the house faces panoramic views to the east. One side of the sitting area also overlooks the swimming pool, protruding from the façade, through picture glass windows. The glass-lined family living room is located on the other side of the pool. Behind the sitting area, a passage leads to the master bathroom. On the west of the second floor, behind the master bedroom, three other bedrooms wrap around the central staircase.

Opposite above and below Visitors can access the swiimming pool via an outdoor staircase. The infinity-edge pool, standing high on stilts, protrudes from the eastern façade. Tall palms pop above its edges. The wood-slatted flooring at the entrance to the family living room continues alongside the pool.

Above A spectacular, illuminated view of the southern (entrance) side of the house showing the oval glass-encased formal living room below and family living room above contained within a rectilinear plan under a massive curved roof.

ario abode

In response to an awkward site, tucked in at a strange angle on a segment of a cul-de-sac in an upscale housing enclave in South Jakarta, architect Sardjono Sani devised a house with three distinct masses. Greeting visitors to the house is a curvilinear mass that follows the curve of the road in front. A smaller oval-shaped mass is placed longitudinally behind it, a little to the right. The third mass, a double-height transparent box, runs perpendicular to the oval, cutting the site into two distinct areas: the enclosed house to the left (west) and a large, open main garden to the right (east). A lap pool, raised above ground, runs longitudinally along the southern edge of the main garden on the side nearest the road. A second garden is placed at the back.

BINTARO, JAKARTA

ARCHITECT SARDJONO SANI
BIAS TEKNO-ART KREASINDO

Above From the pergola at the corner of the house, the raised rectangular pool appears to flow into the garden, which is at a slightly lower level. Palm trees set into the wooden deck provide shade for the pool.

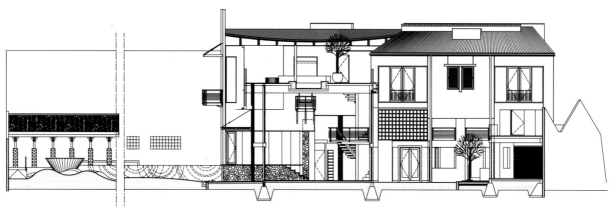

The three masses are arranged in such a way that they intersect with one another at different elevations. They have also been deliberately kept rather narrow in order to allow air and light to effortlessly flow throughout. Tying them together is the main staircase, a radial segment of the curvi-linear mass and the core of the architectural scheme. The play of intersecting masses in this house not only provides an interesting visual and spatial perception, but also allows for the incorporation of the elements of water, light, and wind, making the house comfortable to live in.

Specific functions are generally assigned to the three sections. The half of the oval mass on the first floor facing the garden is designated for private rest and relaxation.

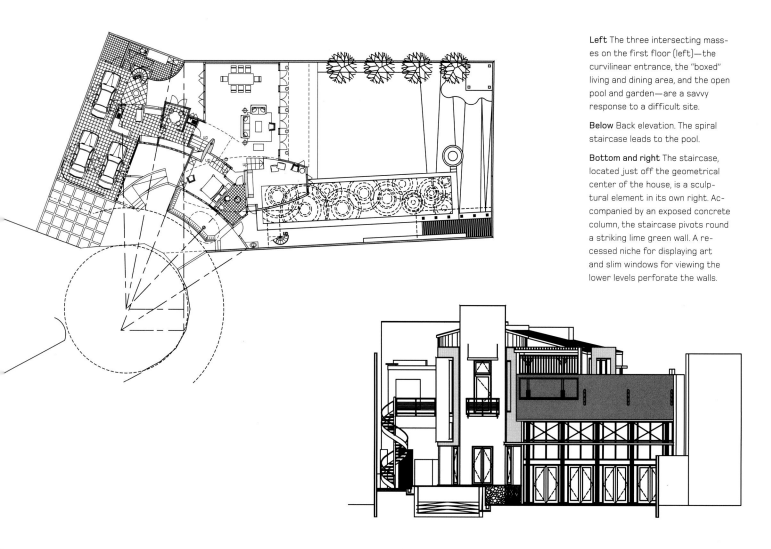

Left The three intersecting masses on the first floor (left)—the curvilinear entrance, the "boxed" living and dining area, and the open pool and garden—are a savvy response to a difficult site.

Below Back elevation. The spiral staircase leads to the pool.

Bottom and right The staircase, located just off the geometrical center of the house, is a sculptural element in its own right. Accompanied by an exposed concrete column, the staircase pivots round a striking lime green wall. A recessed niche for displaying art and slim windows for viewing the lower levels perforate the walls.

while the other half is the family's music/hobby room. The oval on the second floor above is occupied by the master bedroom and adjoining bathroom.

The curvilinear mass is more transitory. On the first floor, the outer terrace and inner foyer of the house occupy the segment facing the street. Behind is the children's play/study room, which faces the secondary garden at the back of the house. The curvilinear mass ends with the service areas and garage at the far left of the site.

The two childrens' bedrooms are placed side by side on the curve on the second floor.

The spatial catalyst and the most public area of the house is the living space housed in the transparent box, which runs the entire height of the house. Here are the main living and dining areas, open to the secondary garden on the left—which also allows for cross-ventilation through the transparent box and the curvilinear mass—and to the main garden and pool on the right.

Left At the end of the dining area, the raised study "floats" over the end of the pool, its transparent laminated glass flooring bringing refracted light into the space.

Above A curved ceramic tile wall in the master bedroom is a perfect foil to the black granite counter, pedestal basin, and flooring.

Right A low-pitched raftered roof laid with planks in the master bedroom harmonizes with the long strips of *bingkirai* wood used on the floor. Clerestory openings above the walls bring in daylight. The stark white walls are a perfect backdrop for modern art.

Below Another section view of the house.

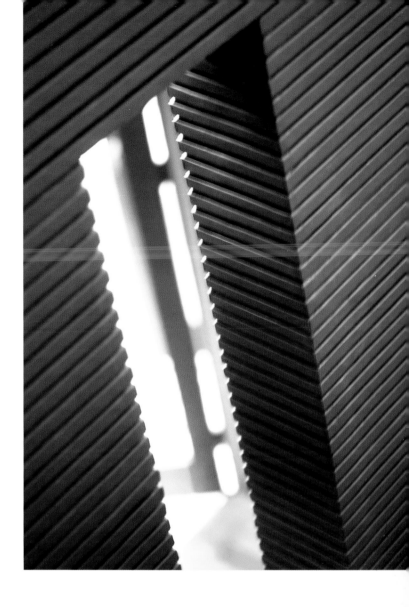

Left A stone urn, specially made with a curved profile to soften the strict lines of the square courtyard, is here viewed from the dining room verandah. The white pebbles bordering the paved courtyard prevent rain splash as well as provide textural contrast.

Right The courtyard is glimpsed through a vertical opening in the grooved plaster wall of the main staircase leading to the bedrooms on the second floor.

k residence

Situated on a medium-sized, elongated, 700-square meter lot, this classic two-story house offers not only a pragmatic but also an aesthetic solution for modern-day living amidst the hustle and bustle of Jakarta.

The dominant feature, indeed the central element, of the house is a double-height inner courtyard placed almost in the exact center of the house. All areas of the house, including the movement of the occupants, revolve around this inner courtyard which is enclosed by full-height, wood-framed windows and doors. A single plant in a simple stone urn is the focus of the paved courtyard. The courtyard allows light to reach every corner of the house, at the same time functioning as a kind of airshaft that provides cross-ventilation and animates air movement throughout all its rooms on both stories.

PONDOK INDAH, JAKARTA

ARCHITECT PATRICK RENDRADJAJA

From the front steps of the house, visitors enter a foyer through double doors, which is spacious enough to show-case the owners' collection of art, before they are led along a warm, wood-floored verandah adjacent to the central inner courtyard, eventually reaching the main living room of the house. Along the way, the deliberate prominence of the inner courtyard is not lost on visitors.

The main living room is placed towards the back of the house on the right. While it has direct access to the inner courtyard through a set of doors placed on one corner, it also opens out to a grassy area at the back of the house, thus extending the entertainment area. It is a spacious, airy, and well-lit space that commands the best views of the house. Overlooking the living room and the courtyard below is a raised dining room. The kitchen at the back of the house, between the living and dining rooms, is concealed by a wine cabinet. At the front of the house, overlooking the street in front and the courtyard behind, is a workspace for the lady of the house, which doubles as a place where guests can be received in an office-like setting. A guest room is placed next to it.

The private spaces of the house are all located on the second floor. The stairs and corridors that lead up to them are highlighted with warm-colored materials and covered with wooden flooring, providing warmth to the areas of house that are meant to be more intimate, in contrast to the use of the rather hard materials and cold colors in the

Opposite above Interior designer Ijus Julius Susanto, responsible for the home's décor, opted for a fusion of trends and materials with an emphasis on comfortable modernism. In the dining room overlooking the courtyard, a white easy-to-maintain statuario marble and stainless steel table is set against a dark floor. The glass wine cabinet conceals the kitchen.

Opposite below A few steps and a white box separate the living room from the dining room. A dark yet warm and intimate *merbau* wood floor further differentiates the space from the other public areas. The floor-to-ceiling doors and low-slung modern furniture add to the spaciousness.

Above Frosted glass sliding doors conceal office equipment and storage in the carefully designed workspace-cum-reception room at the front of the house. The bold andesite stone table pedestals and soft carpet on the granite floor provide tactile and visual contrast in the room.

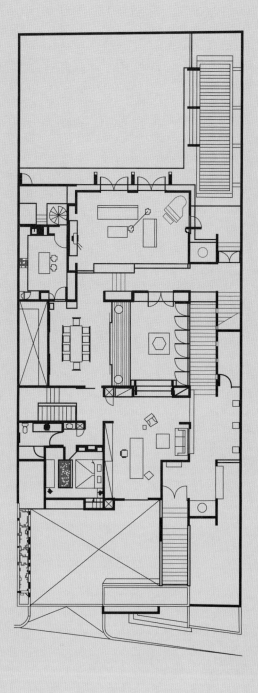

Above left A spiral staircase leads from the children's corner on the second floor to their games room in the attic, where a big window overlooks the entrance foyer.

Left A teak-floored passageway connects the entrance foyer to the living room and the garden terrace beyond. The staircase to the upstairs bedrooms is concealed behind the purple grooved wall, visually connected with the courtyard on the left through narrow vertical openings.

Above The first floor plan shows the central inner courtyard surrounded by a passageway on the right connecting the foyer in front and the private living area and verandah at back. The dining room on the left is adjacent to a void overlooking a small bamboo garden and a workspace adjacent to a guest bedroom at the front.

Above right The curved white ceiling in the master bedroom complements the tones of the dark parquet flooring and yellow wall behind the bed. A large, wood-framed mirror separates the room from the walk-in closet, bathroom, and reading area—which opens out to the balcony overlooking the lawn below.

Right Black and white dominates the color scheme in the main living room. Glimpses of the dining area on the split level, the inner court-yard, and the stairs leading to the bedrooms emphasize the clear separation yet fluidity and con-nectivity of the spaces in the house. The white box does double duty as a divider and storage for the sound system and other items.

Left Bordering the spare back yard covered in fine grass, the verandah is a great place to relax and unwind. The living room on the ground floor and the reading room off the master bedroom above also look out over the lawn.

Below left Shards of light play on the staircase wall and ceiling courtesy of the high windows and the slits in the purple grooved wall.

Below right A striking modern sculpture in the double-height foyer on the right hints at what is to come in the contemporary Indonesian interior. The stone wall on the left separates the andesite stone steps leading to the main entrance from the carport below.

Right The façade of the house from the carport. On the right, a white entrance "hall" with a glass-topped pergola-type roof houses the postbox, doorbell, and intercom. An opening in the back wall leads to the carport, while visitors pass through a steel gate and up the stone stairs. A large overhanging canopy covers the main entrance and the workspace. Wooden louvers screen direct views into the full-height windows of the children's bedrooms upstairs, yet still allow light to enter.

more public areas of the house. Upstairs, the private areas also revolve around the central courtyard and enjoy the light and air flow that it provides.

The master bedroom occupies the space directly to the left of the courtyard void. Beyond it, separated by a huge mirror wall, is a walk-in closet, bathroom, and reading area, the latter opening to a balcony overlooking the back garden. Full-length doors and a balcony off the spacious master bedroom also allow views of the courtyard below. The two children's rooms are located side by side at the front of the house. A games room, accessed by a spiral staircase, occupies the front right.

steel house

BEKASI, JAKARTA

ARCHITECT AHMAD DJUHARA
DJUHARA+DJUHARA

In recent years, modern architectural design has largely been the prerogative of an élite upper middle-class clientele. The scene is slowly changing, however, as young Indonesian architects—and their emerging middle-class clients—develop a taste for the simplicity and clarity of modern design and the efficiency of twenty-first century methods of construction, as well as an awareness of the convenience and comfort of living in such a home. More and more modernistic designs are thus starting to dot the urban landscape in middle-income neighborhoods.

Ahmad Djuhara's Steel House, located in the midst of a modest housing estate in Bekasi, just east of Jakarta, offers a stark yet handsome middle-class housing alternative in present-day Indonesia. Through a compact and efficient design program constructed with recycled building materials, the architect managed to resolve the spatial and budgetary limitations which were major issues in the project.

In dealing with a limited site measuring less than 120 square meters with a nine-meter-wide frontage, the architect challenged—successfully—the rigid four-meter setback

Left The exposed diagonal tie rods bracing the steel frame form an aesthetic element on the ground floor of the house. The geometry of the white ceramic floor tiles inside harmonizes well with the plaster floor pattern outside.

Below left The south elevation of the house.

Below While a trellis in front of the site and a low wall at the end of the dining area shield the front of the house from views from the street, the glass walls of the house allow the interior to visually extend out to the driveway.

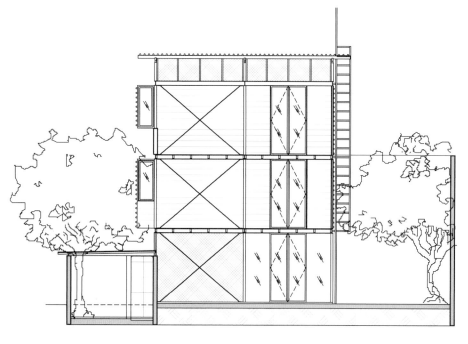

regulations imposed by the municipal government in the area. He argued that if the setback regulations allowed for the provision of security guard posts in élite houses, they should also allow for the provision of staff and service quarters in middle-income housing. The main structure of the house, which basically appears as a six square meter glass and steel cube erected on steel stilts, is thus placed in the middle of the site, adjacent to a car porch on the left (east), and with a relatively spacious four by nine meter open garden at the rear (south).

The design of the house is based on the most fundamental requirements of modern-day middle-class living, and these have been addressed by offering efficiency, both spatially as well as in terms of construction. On each of the floors of the three-story building, the right (west) side, which retains more heat during the day, is reserved for services. This arrangement also allows for the creation of spacious open living rooms on the left side, which is more exposed to the morning sun, and commands views of the open garden at the back. The use of recycled steel as the main building material, in combination with precast bricks, contributed to efficiency in construction time, labor, and materials, compared with the use of concrete, the most common building material used in the area, which would have required larger structural dimensions, longer setting and construction time, higher labor costs, and would have

Far left The kitchen, dining, and living spaces are positioned to maximize the small floor area. The color orange indicates the service areas of the house. A kitchen counter clad in orange-stained wood separates the open kitchen from the dining room. Hidden behind the orange wall is the staircase and storage area.

Left The living room opens up to the back yard, contained within a tall wall, which allows extra entertainment space.

Below left The master bedroom on the third floor is an enclosed, tranquil retreat. Openings are limited to a couple of relatively small swing windows at one end.

Right Lightness and simplicity, achieved by an unorthodox combination of steel structure, corrugated zinc sheets, and transparent glass, are the hallmarks of Ahmad Djuhara's Steel House.

Below The first floor plan (below) shows the linear arrangement of the house, with the car porch on the left, the main living areas in the center, and the service areas on the right. The servant's quarters and laundry drying area in front are enclosed by a wall and trellis. In the third floor plan (above), the master bedroom and sitting area, and attached bathroom, occupy the entire space.

also produced more construction waste. Conscious that the heat-retaining metals might not be deemed suitable for use in the tropics, the architect used corrugated zinc sheets on a steel frame to create a plenum placed over the structure of the building to shield it from heat.

On the first floor of the Steel House, the staircase, kitchen, and storeroom are placed on the right of the space, adjacent to the perimeter wall, allowing for a voluminous living and dining area which opens out to the carport on the left and the open garden behind. The servant's room and laundry jut out, in line with the kitchen, towards the front of the site, while the servant's bedroom and bathroom and the laundry drying area, which is concealed by a low vertical trellis, are placed in front of the site.

The front half of the second floor is divided equally into three single bedrooms for the children, arranged side by side in a row. The walls of the bedrooms facing the street are made of corrugated zinc sheets, peeled out in such a way as to protect the rooms from outside noise while creating small openings at the ends for the entry of morning sun. The three bedrooms open out to a large television-cum-living room at the back half of the floor. A shared bathroom is on the right, next to the staircase.

The master bedroom takes up the entire third floor of the house. The roomy space—the size of the children's floor below and the dining, living and kitchen areas on the first floor—is filled with a bed, sitting/television area, and a simple walk-in closet and dressing area which lead to a modest bathroom. The room looks over the paved driveway on the left and the garden at the back.

This stark and simple structure has become an architectural expression that incorporates Louis Sullivan's maxim of "form follows function" and Mies van der Rohe's "less is more," as well as the most fundamental principles of modern architectural design and construction. Djuhara's Steel House has justifiably become a statement that modern functional design has a lot to offer to the modern middle class living in Indonesia today.

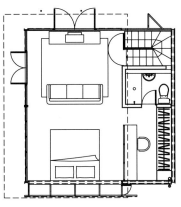

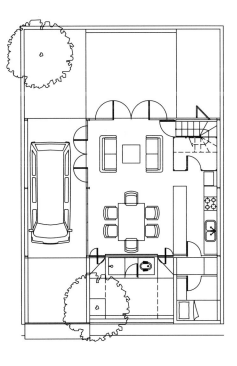

y house

PONDOK INDAH, JAKARTA

ARCHITECTS JUDI WANANDI & COSMAS GOZALI
ARCHITELIER

The design of this seemingly "inverted" home is a clear attempt to break free of the usual house design conventions. A volume of planes with small openings on the lower part, but large ones above, greets the visitor. The main entrance to the house is moved to the right (east) of the site, freeing the façade of any doors except for the roll-up garage door. Only after circumambulating the volume on two sides, via a paved pathway running from the driveway along the front of the house, does the visitor reach the main door of the house.

On entering the double-height foyer, it quickly becomes apparent that the house is composed of two large volumes, with the entrance foyer placed in between. The back volume, its upper part painted light blue, is set off at a slight angle from the front volume, which is painted light green all over. Visible to the visitor at the entrance is a ramped bridge that connects the two volumes, and a staircase that leads to the second floor of the front volume. The main circulation of the house is thus concentrated in this intermediary space, its lightness and transparency—

and the effect of being outside while already inside the house—enhanced by the generous use of steel, glass, and wood, including a transparent glass roof. The two volumes thus become the inside proper of the house.

The functions of the house oscillate between the two volumes. To the north of the entrance on the first floor is the main open-plan living and dining space, its walls painted a soft yellow to match the color of the wall at the entrance side of the foyer. The living and dining room, together with an adjoining kitchen and pantry, faces the garden at the back of the house.

Originating from the dining area, the staircase leads to the second floor of the front volume, where a sitting room and guest room are placed. The bedroom is treated as another box that projects out of the front volume, like a drawer that has been slightly pulled out. The sitting room, surrounded by tall windows on two sides, forms a well-lit sunroom. A ramp connects the sitting room to the main bedroom of the house, which occupies the entire back volume. A staircase inside the room leads to an interior mezzanine which is used as a study. The windows extend the full double height of the bedroom, flooding it with light during the day and providing views to the garden at the back.

Throughout the house, simple, elegant furniture is offset by colorful modern paintings and accessories.

Above left Simple furniture and modern art by Sunaryo, Srihadi Soedarsono, and Dolorosa Sinagais blend beautifully with the clean architectural lines of the living/dining area adjoining the checkered foyer. Old wooden door and window railings grace the walls.

Above right The first, second, and third (roof) plans of the house.

Right Brilliant red flowers and cushions, and a striking painting by young artist Gusbarlian brighten up the living room with its quiet arrangement of simple dark sofa set and metal-framed, honey-colored, molded plywood tables.

Above left The slatted ramp above the foyer, topped by the skylight, leads to the master bedroom.

Above right The steel frames of the dining chairs curve elegantly in contrast to the rigid construction of the powder-coated steel and glass dining table. The living/dining area opens out to a small garden at the back of the house.

Right From the sitting area, a blind-covered window allows the occupants to monitor the arrival of guests at the front door.

Opposite Modern reproductions of Le Corbusier's Petite Comfort love seat and chair dominate the sitting room on the second level of the south volume. Doors lead to a small patio above the garage.

Above The ramp leading from the sitting room on the upper level of the south volume to the master bedroom in the north volume complements the wood-paneled storage cupboard at one end of the sitting room and the door of the bedroom. Stylish floor lamps make a strong statement in the otherwise simply decorated space.

Left Another view of the bridging ramp under a skylight between the two volumes, hovering over the entrance foyer. Old wood-carved statues form a reception committee at the front door.

Opposite above The master bedroom opens to a small garden at the back of the house. A painting by Singaporean artist Teng Nee Cheong enlivens the simple room furnished only with a large king-sized bed with a wooden headboard and side table, a pair of ottomans at the foot, and Ron Arad's fancy Tom Vac chair.

Opposite below The foyer is a tactile and visual delight with its mixture of smooth black and white checkered floor tiles, wooden staircase slats, framed wooden house railings, and yellow and blue paintwork..

tantowi residence

JEFFREY BUDIMAN & ILHAM N.

In designing the residence of Indonesia's leading television presenter and host of the Indonesian edition of the "Who Wants To Be A Millionaire" game show, Tantowi Yahya, architect Jeffrey Budiman maintained his architectural maxim of creating highly livable spaces within a relatively modest enclosure. "After all, a house should be enjoyed when spending time living inside it, not from the outside. There is little use in flaunting a flashy exterior, especially during times like this in Indonesia," the architect explains.

The Tantowi residence, situated in the middle-class neighborhood of Bintaro, thus appears unassuming from the outside. Set on a plateau raised above the level of the road, the hipped roof house is almost invisible from the

BINTARO, JAKARTA

ARCHITECTS JEFFREY BUDIMAN & ILHAM N. J. BUDIMAN ARCHITECTS

Above Elevated above the road, a large rectangular swimming pool screened by a low slate wall greets visitors to the house. A rich variety of materials, colors, and textures are used to treat the walls and floors of the pool plaza, including the portico leading to the guest room to the right of the pool.

Above left Clusters of comfortable chairs and sofas are interspersed with a dark glass-top coffee table and matching dining set in the main living and dining room, sandwiched between the entrance plaza in front and the garden behind. A few well-chosen artifacts complement the tones of the furnishings.

Above A wall of decorative terra-cotta blocks created by artist Teguh Ostenrik, their irregular surface highlighted by four lamps suspended from a girder over the dining table, adds color and warmth to the dining/living space. Blinds on both sets of doors afford transparency as well as privacy.

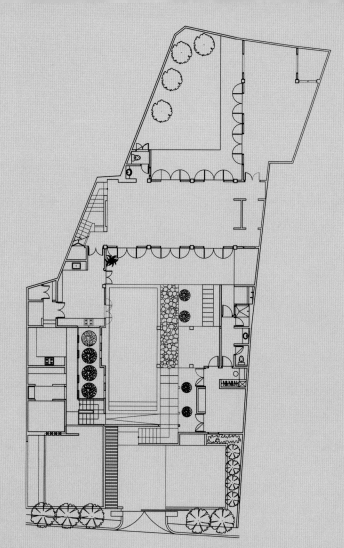

Above left A reproduction of Le Corbusier's chaise longue forms a comfortable reading chair in the music room. A small terrace at the corner of the site brings additional light into the room.

Above right The first (ground) floor plan of the house shows the irregular composition of spaces around the pool. The main house volume lies between the pool plaza in front and the garden and courtyard at the back.

Left A comfortable chair on the porch outside the guest bedroom is a wonderful place to relax and view the pool, plants, and artifacts decorating the plaza area. Water-resistant hardwood planks are both warm and safe to walk on.

Above right The music room on the far right corner of the site is dominated by a built-in display cabinet holding Tantowi's collection of guitars, a television set and audio-visual system below it, and photographs and other mementoes on the side shelves.

Right An old wooden artifact mounted on a wall of horizontal stacked slate makes a stunning centerpiece in the master bedroom. The smoothness of the parquet flooring is a delightful contrast to the coarse texture of the stacked slate, the white slatted doors, and the pattern on the rug.

street. What is visible is a low wall retaining the raised elevation, which also acts as a barrier against the eyes of passers-by. Only after ascending the steps that cut into a small opening in the wall do visitors realize that they have entered the compound and can see the house. From the top of the steps, the inside and outside spaces open up, flowing and merging fluidly, echoing the eloquence and warmth of the owner and his family.

The architectural elements are organized on the site in such a way that their irregular placement is barely noticeable. The main building is strategically placed in the middle of the site, behind the pool, just where the layout of the house starts to slant to the right. At the same time, it divides the open spaces of the house into two: a larger entrance courtyard dominated by the swimming pool in front, and a smaller garden at the back of the house. The more formal entrance courtyard draws visitors to the living and dining area, strategically placed between the two open spaces. Beyond, to the right and also facing the back garden, is Tantowi's hobby room, which houses his collection of guitars and music paraphernalia. On the far corner of the hobby room is another smaller courtyard.

Left The swimming pool and its surrounding plaza take center stage in the Tantowi house and are a perfect backdrop for relaxing, cooling down, exercising, al-fresco dining, entertaining, or simply as a reflective artistic feature of the house. A piano at one corner of the porch, adjacent to the open-plan living room, is ideally placed for entertaining, while ample seating around the pool allows for contemplation. Beautiful old objects make a dramatic visual statement. The children's bedrooms on the second floor have commanding views of the pool through large, painted, wood-framed glass openings.

Above The low structure on the other side of the pool facing the guest bedroom annex accom-modates the service areas of the house, including a pantry where the family can enjoy a quick break-fast or a meal by the pool. For more formal dining, the adjacent living-cum-dining room is easily accessed from both the kitchen and the pantry.

The service areas of the house—kitchen, laundry, and storage—are arranged to the left of the entrance courtyard. To the right of the pool is a guest room fronted by a portico. A stairway providing vertical circulation is placed in the triangular-shaped space between the service areas and the main building.

The bedrooms are arranged on the second story of the main building. Although the master bedroom faces the inner garden, it also has access to the entrance courtyard and pool. As Tantowi's children are still relatively young, the children's rooms are placed adjoining the master bed-room, with a connecting door providing direct access from the master bedroom to the room of the younger child.

The Tantowi House is composed of relatively thin masses cross-secting the site to offer not only a flowing progression of spaces but also other environmental facilities. The three open spaces of the house channel sunlight into the spaces, while the differential air pressure they create causes fresh air to flow throughout the house, making it cool and airy even on a day when the Jakarta sun is blazing hot. Comfort in the Tantowi house is achieved through the use of a simple and logical architectural composition.

amanda house

Left Lime green and burnt orange are used as accents throughout the house: on external walls, in upholstery and cushions, in flower arrangements, and in this cupboard and sofa placed in front of the exposed concrete wall shielding the central staircase.

Right A mixture of four colors—lime green, burnt orange, white, and brown—set against a variety of textures—steel, wood, stone, and vegetation—enhance the *kampung* atmosphere of this house, as shown by the entrance.

Imposing palatial houses with pseudo-historical styles such as double-height Corinthian columns crowned with Mansard roofs dominate the élite Pondok Indah housing estate in South Jakarta. Among its upper middle-class occupants, the idea of space and spaciousness is largely determined by the built-up area. As a result, most houses in the estate occupy as much of the land area as possible, with little consideration given to the environmental surroundings.

Amongst Pondok Indah's "concrete jungle" there do, however, remain some sites with pleasant panoramic views of the heavily wooded surroundings, such as the corner site on which this house is built. The sloping site is bordered on two sides by a road at the bottom. A river runs through a valley further east. To take full advantage of this splendid setting, the owners requested a design in which the natural surroundings could be seen and appreciated.

Impressed by the sweeping views to the east, architect Irianto PH responded by creating a multiple split-level house that followed the slope of the site, its spaces connected by a large staircase in the middle of the house that

PONDOK INDAH, JAKARTA

ARCHITECT IRIANTO PH
ANTARA DESIGN

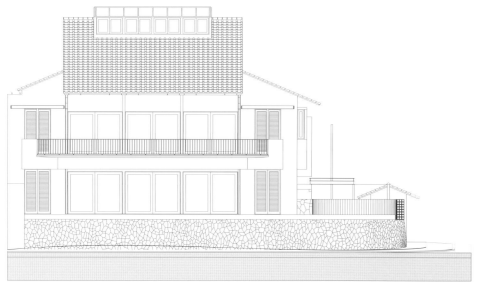

Above and below right An eclectic mix of orange upholstered sofas, rattan chairs cushioned in off-white, and simple wood furniture in the main living room on the lower level complements the dominant architectural colors. A built-in cabinet enclosing a television set emerges from a granite ledge in front of the exposed concrete wall that extends from the lower to the upper level of the house, shielding the staircase.

Left The east elevation, showing the timber-framed glass doors covering the upper and lower level living rooms, and the tall hip roof, equipped with a skylight, crowning the house.

Above right Handsome timber-framed glass doors installed on floor pivots on three sides of the living room allow the ceramic tile flooring of the living room to continue smoothly out to the terrace, thus forming one continuous space. The balustrade of the upper level terrace, constructed of metal, protrudes over the wall of the living room, forming a small canopy and protecting the openings below from rain.

functions as a light-cum-air stairwell. The house is thus a fractured composition of levels and platforms in which space and spaciousnesss are not defined by the floor area but by the extent of the interrelationships among the spaces and their environmental surroundings.

The most prominent spaces of the house are two living room platforms on the first and second levels from which the views can be enjoyed. To the left of the staircase are bedrooms on each of the two levels. On the third level, to the south of the house, is the master bedroom, while the area below it on the ground floor is occupied by the dining room and kitchen. The garage is located in the basement.

The house is entered via an unusual circular concrete ramp that brings visitors from the sunken entrance gate up to the main entrance to the house on the first floor. On this level, to the left of the entrance, the spacious living room platform extends out beyond a set of pivoting glass doors to a terrace and further on to the lawn in one continuous plane. The inside and outside are united by means of this continuous surface. Even though it terminates at the edge of the lot where the grass drops, the grass edge seems to extend visually on to the surroundings, much like an infinity-edge pool. On the second floor, the living room platform is extended out by means of a tapered concrete slab. The slab, kept thin and left exposed, and without supporting beams, provides a protective cover for the large openings of the lower level living room, at the same time leaving the elevation simple and uncluttered.

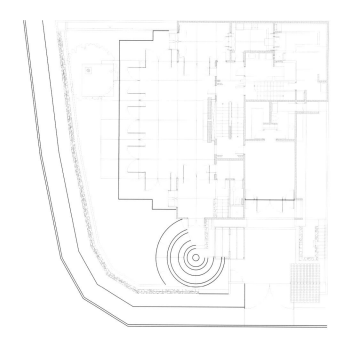

Above The first floor plan shows the relationship of the house to the corner lot. Entry is via a circular concrete ramp.

Below from left to right Adjustable fins on the steel entrance canopy (left) control the entry of sun and rain. A skylight above the staircase (center) brings light into the house. Lights set into the wall (right) illuminate the steps at the bottom of the main stairwell.

Right The orange wood-lined and railed staircase is the central element in the house, providing access to the various staggered levels. Screening the stairwell from the living room is an exposed concrete wall imprinted with a pattern of planks, complementing the other natural materials used. The wall stops just short of the full height of the ceiling of the second floor living room.

villa cibulan

FARIED MASDOEKI & KUSUMA AGUSTIANTO

Situated on a large piece of land overlooking the rolling hills in the mountainous region of Puncak, West Java, this modern villa serves as an escape from the hustle and bustle of Jakarta, about two hours' drive away.

Reminiscent of Indonesia's traditional longhouse typology, the house is designed as a simple composition of longitudinal boxes, one stacked on top of the other, in order to maximize views of the surrounding valley and hills. The two boxes are sheltered by a simple gable roof, which appears to be supported by a series of columns that run around the periphery of the smaller, enclosed box on the upper level and extend down to the ground, penetrating the larger ground level box.

CIBULAN, WEST JAVA

ARCHITECTS FARIED MASDOEKI & KUSUMA AGUSTIANTO
GRAHACIPTA HADIPRANA

Above The design of the villa makes full use of the expansive horizontal site, maximizing views of the mountain range behind. While the main structure of the house comprises three masses—a central mass flanked by two others— additional masses and planes protrude from the main structure.

Extending out of the longitudinal composition on the western side of the site, facing the road, is a supporting structure that includes the entrance, staircase, a guest room, and the servant's quarters. While this structure is imporant in providing access to the house, giving additional space, and linking the two stories, it also helps to buffer the house from the noise emanating from the heavily trafficked Pun-cak road beyond, one of the major thoroughfares connect-ing Jakarta and Bandung. Massive walls on this side of the house further protect the villa from noise and traffic fumes. In complete contrast, the opposite side of the villa is quiet and secluded, opening completely out to the east, where the owners and their guests can enjoy the scenery.

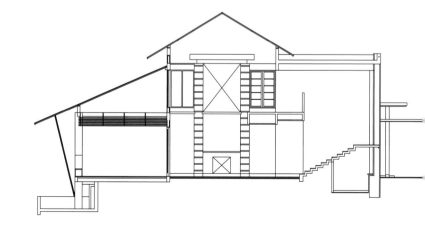

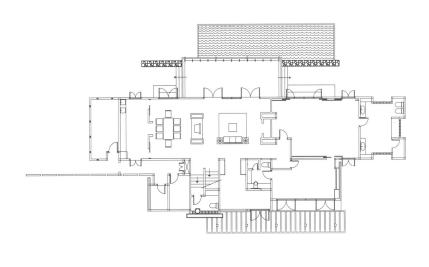

Opposite above and above Reminiscent of a loosely draped Balinese *gringsing* cloth, "Pesona Gringsing" by Ribut Suwarsono, installed above the volcanic stone fireplace, emphasizes the verticality of the double-height living room. Mirroring the fireplace at the opposite end is a large latticed cupboard concealing the television.

Opposite below Section view.

Top First floor plan (above) and elevation (below).

Left A large painting of three young Balinese men by Wayan Bawa Antara and a Balinese sculpture enhance the entranceway.

Left The house's timber theme is carried through to the ceiling, floor, balustrades, and doors in the second floor corridors leading to the bedrooms. The airy void above the living room moderates the "denseness" of the practical wood finishes.

Above from left to right Spiraling cones used to raise the glass table top (left) form an interesting visual play with the cones carved into the wood below. An embossed stone wall at the landing of the staircase (center) adds tactile and visual contrast. Cream marble combined with a dark trim makes a strong graphic statement in the bathroom (right).

Below A large cupboard holding a television set on one side and storage on the other separates the living and dining areas.

Left The main entrance doors to the villa are flanked by two dark columns resting under the canopy of the portico.

Below Rounded columns rise above the podium of the lower level to support the roof, reminiscent of the architectural composition of Donald Friend's main house in Batu Jimbar, Bali, designed by Geoffrey Bawa. While in Bawa's composition the upper level is left open like a traditional Balinese pavilion, here, unusually, the upper story is fully enclosed behind the columns.

Above right The living room opens out to a terracotta-tiled terrace framing beautiful views of the mountainous valley. Part of the roof is a skylight to allow plenty of light into the house.

Below right Columnar fountain heads circulate water in one of the pools around the house.

Inside, the longitudinal composition of the house is broken into three distinct parts by four large concrete piers which extend the entire two-story height. On the ground level, the central section of the house, defined by the four piers, accommodates the living room. At one end is a fireplace for cool nights, set between two piers. A large wooden terrace extends from the living room into the gardens, providing a warm space to enjoy the views of the valley. The terrace also provides a transition from the controlled environment of the villa to the vast open space. The master bedroom is placed to the right of the central piers, in the south wing, while the dining room is located in the left (north) wing of the house, together with the kitchen and a utilities room at the very end of the structure.

The smaller box on the upper level houses a guest bedroom, fashioned as a luxurious and spacious hotel suite, which covers the entire north wing. The south wing accommodates a study and an open terrace, which extends out beyond the roofline of the house to the unsheltered roof deck of the ground level box. A passageway bordered by wooden balconies runs along three sides of the central void overlooking the living room below.

Left A wooden balcony protrudes from the upper level of the large central house, supported by a concrete beam that frames the back entrance. A large old tree helps shield the house from views across the creek which cuts through the middle of the site.

Right Thin planes of concrete and glass and sun-catching "flaps" on the roof are innovative solutions to the entry of light and air on the narrow, wedge-shaped site.

howard house

KEBAYORAN BARU, JAKARTA

ARCHITECTS BUDIMAN HENDROPURNOMO
& DICKY HENDRASTO
DENTON CORKER MARSHALL PTY LTD

A new complex comprising a large central house (shown here) and nine townhouses has been developed on a triangular-shaped residential site formerly owned by the embassy of the German Democratic Republic. Five houses had been built on the area bordered by the street in front and the natural Krukuk creek behind, which cuts longitudinally through the middle of the site. A kindergarten had occupied the triangular site across the creek. The architecture of the old houses, dating from the late 1960s, featured some interesting design elements of the time, such as outward-slanting walls, popularly known as the *jengki* style (see page 15), and white slate arranged in graphic patterns on the lower parts of the outer walls.

Despite the rather interesting design of the old structures, technical problems meant they had to be torn down. However, the location of the architects' nine new townhouses is literally based on the footprint of the five old houses, with three new townhouses inserted in gaps in between the five, and with one of the houses divided to become two townhouses. The design of the new townhouses was intended to evoke memories of the old houses rather than to physically mimic them. The slanted walls

Left A colorful painting by Teguh Ostenrik brightens the almost monochromatic palette of the living room on the ground floor and the circulation corridors above bordering the void.

Below The dining area, placed strategically next to the kitchen, overlooks the gardens. The large glass-topped dining table combines beautifully with a set of lightweight chairs of molded plywood and stainless steel.

Right The bright and seamless living room is the center of the house, its concrete columns soaring to the sun-catching forms above, its glass wall openings bringing in views of the outside.

appear again in the nine new townhouses, as does the cladding, but this time round dark gray slate is arranged in horizontal layers. Due to the availability of new materials, a completely different approach was adopted for the gable roofs, which appear to have a light "blanket" laid over them as a protective shield against sun and rain. At the front (west) of the site, an opening leads to a common service area for the nine townhouses. From here, following the old plan, a bridge connects the front of the site to the back (east).

Across the bridge, a lush garden provides a pleasant transition between the creek and the new main house, illustrated here, which is placed in the V-shaped wedge on the east side of the triangle. The house is laid out as a series of rectangular boxes running parallel to the creek, starting from a long, thin, rectangular box on the creek side to wider but shorter boxes towards the back.

The rectangular boxes placed on the left (south) of the site, adjacent to the creek, contain the service areas of the

house—the garage, guards' and servants' quarters, laundry room, and kitchen—while also serving as a protective birm alongside the creek. The rest of the house takes shape towards the right side, where the site is wider before it tapers to a triangular point at the north end. While the service birm shields the main house from the townhouses on the west bank of the river, an old tree provides an additional screen, protecting the main house from the outside.

The most distinctive architectural feature of the house is its roof. Formed of thin concrete, it appears like a series of flexible flaps that have been lifted up to to form an elegant curve, allowing for openings on the raised side of the flaps. The curvilinear "sun catchers" redirect the sun's rays and provide indirect light inside the building. The main sun catcher hovers over the long and narrow double-height living space, while five smaller ones are placed over the games room and the three bedrooms on the second story. They allow light to enter all the rooms even though the windows are shielded with curtains.

Left and right The swimming pool below the "tail" of the house was designed to appear to meander into the site from the creek. The wood planks on the deck are echoed on the ceiling, which is dotted with lights for nighttime swimming. The profiles of the Acupunto chairs, designed by father and son team Yos and Leonard Theosabrata, harmonize perfectly with the curving pool.

Below The staircase connecting the first and second floors turns towards the "spine" of the house at the back of the site, visible through the full-length windows.

Below right The plans of the first (below) and second (above) floors show the location of the house on its wedge-shaped site to the east of the Krukuk creek. The service areas on the first floor are to the left (south), while the house proper occupies the triangular section to the right (north).

The dining area occupies one side of the double-height living room, outfitted in comfortable chairs and modern paintings, while the master bedroom, with a study above it, occupies the other side. An internal staircase in the master bedroom allows the occupants to reach the oval-shaped audio-visual room on the second floor without having to step out of the room on the ground level or use the main staircase of the house.

A casual sitting and music area, located at one end of the living room, continues out to a wood-floored terrace, swimming pool, and the gardens beyond. The azure swimming pool appears to emerge from the creek, entering the grounds on the right-hand corner of the house, before meandering into the wood-covered terrace. The impression that the pool emerges from the creek is further enhanced by the use of a ramp, rather than steps, for a gentle transition rather than a sudden drop from the terrace into the pool. A fish pond in the garden in front of the dining room, adjacent to the river, is the architect's attempt to incorporate another river element into the site.

A staircase between the dining and living spaces leads to the rooms on the second floor. Along the main "spine," one bedroom is set at the "head," facing the front of the house, while a games room and another bedroom are arranged at the "tail," raised on pilotis above the swimming pool and gardens.

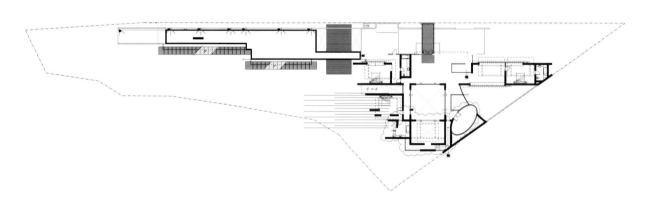

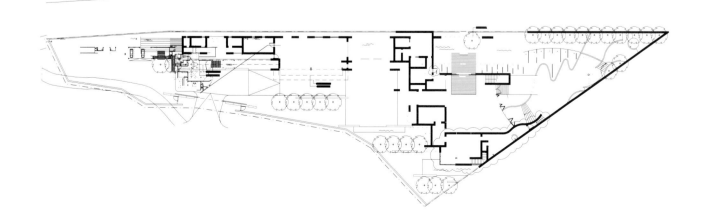

tirtawisata house

Left Tall "fountain" grass not only masks the structure of the garage below it and the reflecting pool in front of the terrace but also filters views into the living room and enlivens the monochromatic paintwork on the exterior.

Right In contrast to the cube's stark white and pale gray walls, architectural elements outside the house employ dark colors: large gray stone pavers, andesit *candi* stone walls, and a dark-stained *merbau* wood gate.

Overleaf Large windows on both sides of the living room—shorter on the west side to reduce heat from the sun's rays—create a play of inside–outside. The living room enjoys views of the grass garden on one side and the pool on the other. The transparent glass floor bordering the pool side brings light into the dining room below.

PERMATA BUANA, JAKARTA

ARCHITECTS ANTONY LIU & FERRY RIDWAN
DWITUNGGAL MANDIRI

Halfway through building a house mimicking the so-called Mediterranean style popular among the upper middle class of Jakarta, house owner Dharma Tirtawisata met architect Antony Liu. Impressed by Liu's modernist architectural designs, he asked the architect to reconfigure his house under construction. Although work on the house had, by this time, reached the second floor, Liu agreed to redesign the house, salvaging what he could of the earlier blueprints. The result is a bold, light-colored concrete and glass cubist sculpture which combines comfort and flexibility with dramatic impact. Vertical sunshades and concrete balconies relieve the starkness of the exterior, along with judiciously placed outdoor "gardens." Inside, contemporary materials— concrete, glass, stone, wood—are used in a bold but neutral palette. The materials, embellishments, and furnishings together portray restrained elegance.

Above left and right Functional minimalism—"less is more"—defines the sparse dining room next to the pool. An extra-long modernist table set against clean walls and floors dominates the space. Light shines through the double-height openings on the pool side and from the transparent glass floor above.

Left Designed for adaptability, the study on the third floor can easily be converted into another bedroom, its built-in armoire serving as a wardrobe.

The architect's first task, in conjunction with colleague Ferry Ridwan, was to free the house from the use of a conventional gable roof, thus allowing him to plan a new geometry: a three-story house composed of two slightly unequal rectangles, one rectangle shifted to the front to allow for an above-ground swimming pool at the back left corner of the site. A staircase, placed almost exactly in the middle of the house, serves as a spatial pivot as well as a connector for the two rectangles.

Although at first glance the house resembles a some-what strange shoebox, it is, in fact, a complex structure encased within rectangular planes of walls, the side walls covered in *paras* limestone, the remainder plastered naturally

or painted a light gray. The planes are cut out at certain places for openings that allow light and views into the rooms. The void above the swimming pool on the first floor acts as a lightwell that brings sunlight into all three floors of the house. The dining room on the first floor, the living room on the second floor, and the bedrooms on the third floor of the house all face the swimming pool and benefit from this light tunnel. One side of the living room floor is formed of transparent reinforced glass to further allow light to filter into the level below. The design of the house thus organizes the spaces in a pragmatic manner, and at the same time restructures the way light interacts with the spaces.

Opposite above left Dark-stained full-length wardrobes form abundant storage along a corridor tucked behind the wall of the master bedroom and can be entered from either side.

Opposite above right Transparent glass meets Citatah marble in this stunning floor in the living room.

Opposite below left A shard of light from a slit in the canopy plays on the bold black bathtub offset by light-colored walls and flooring.

Opposite below right Aluminum louvers on all levels of the house moderate light and air. The marble floor demarcates the living room seating area.

Above A platform bed flanked by two tall Japanese lamps is the focal point in the master bedroom. The wall behind conceals the full-length wardrobes and the passageway to the bathroom.

Right The front elevation (above) and side elevation (below) indicate the cubist theme of the big bold house.

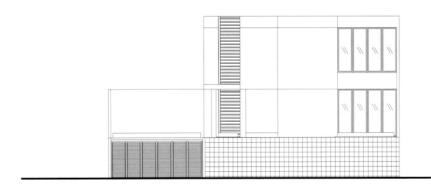

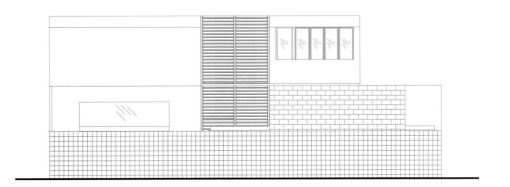

Above Overlooking the "fountain" grass on the garage roof garden, the guest bedroom on the third floor does double duty as a gallery. Teguh Ostenrik's large bronze sculpture, "As a Rock," makes a bold statement among the simple modern furniture.

Right The plans of the first floor (above) and second floor (below) show the position of the two slightly unequal rectangles, with the central staircase serving as a spatial pivot and connector. The dining room on the first floor, the living room on the second, and the two bedrooms on the third all face the swimming pool and receive light from its void.

Opposite above What looks like a two-story building is actually three. At night, uplights highlight the second and third floors.

Opposite below The terrace on the second floor acts as a transition area between the inside and out. Here, the dark and coarse materials of the exterior meet the smooth and light-colored surfaces of the interior.

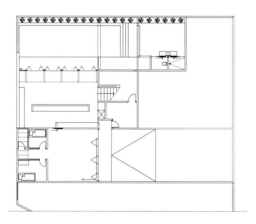

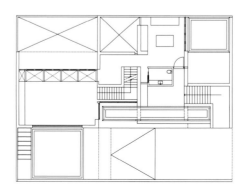

The house is entered via a small terrace on the second floor at the top of a flight of stairs leading from the driveway. A longitudinal reflecting pool buffers the entrance from the driveway. Beyond the entrance, the second floor acts as a kind of *piano nobile*, and it is here that the semi-public spaces are located. This floor is largely taken up with the formal living room, which enjoys an exclusive view, on one side, of the highly unusual grass "garden" above the garage and, on the other side, the swimming pool through full-height glass windows. An informal living room also occupies this floor.

The central staircase leads down to the service areas of the house on the first floor, including the garage, which is partly submerged below the grass roof garden, and the longitudinal above-ground swimming pool, enclosed on two sides by a high block wall. The rectangular dining room opens out to the pool through tall glass doors. Adjacent to it is the kitchen. At the narrow end of the pool is an exercise room.

The private areas of the house, including the master bedroom, a guest bedroom-cum-gallery, and a study, are all placed on the third floor of the house, again accessed by the central staircase.

inke gallery house

MENTENG, JAKARTA

DESIGNER YUSMAN SISWANDI
DEYA PRODUCT DESIGN

Left A brick wall laid in a unique pattern gives character to the house and makes a wonderful backdrop for the display of finely crafted objects.

Right A "floating" staircase of concrete steps with wood treads cantilevered from the structural wall leads from the gallery on the second floor to another gallery on the third. The unfinished quality of the walls and stairs harmonizes beautifuly with the pottery on display on the wooden table below.

Local zoning regulations in the buffer zone between the high-rise business district along Jakarta's main boulevard, Jalan MH Thamrin, and the low-rise élite and historical residential neighborhood of Menteng allow mid-rise development for offices or commercial use. While Menteng is a residential district with strict conservation restrictions, buildings up to four stories can be constructed within the buffer zone. Taking full advantage of this, designer Yusman Siswandi, who also owns the small site, planned a building with multiple functions: a display gallery, a private house, and an office. Essentially, the building is a modern-day take on the traditional shophouse, degraded in most developments towards the end of the twentieth century, but here forming a strategically located, easily accessible workplace within the home that not only reduces travel time between home and workplace but also provides liveability, comfort, and aesthetics along with efficiency and functionality.

The designer's conscious attempt to conform to the architectural character of historical Menteng, which is dotted with a number of public buildings built between the 1930s and

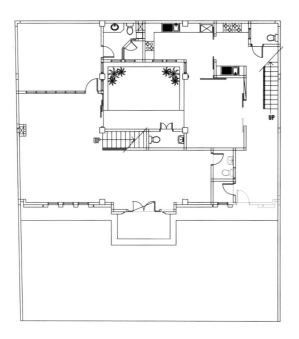

Top On the first floor, the gallery areas wrap around two sides of the central courtyard, with the kitchen and dining room at right.

Above A clerestory window in the double-height entrance foyer brings in light from the front. While the door is finely hand-crafted, the walls of the space are made to appear unfinished.

Above An esoteric and eclectic mix of objects, some newly crafted, others elegant decaying antiques, provide a glimpse of what the gallery house is all about. A simple chandelier composed of lights installed around a circular band of tempered steel ceremoniously embellishes the space.

1950s, is evident in the building's Art Deco proportions and the emphasis on craftsmanship. Although the detailing, particularly the latticed woodwork on the façade and the brickwork of the walls, is reminiscent of Frank Lloyd Wright, Yusman also looked to Indonesia's long tradition of working in terracotta and wood. The brickwork alludes to the terracotta temples of Java, particularly those built during the Majapahit era, while the woodwork is similar to that found on various traditional houses throughout Indonesia, particularly the Toraja houses of Sulawesi.

Surrounded by high-rise buildings, the house, which is pushed back to the boundaries on three sides, covers the entire buildable 220 square meters of the 335-square meter site, allowing for a seven-meter setback in front.

The organizing element of the three-story building is a sky-lit void-cum-courtyard, extending the complete height of the building, around which the living and gallery spaces are arranged. The central void allows air to flow through the building, while distributing light to the rooms during the day. An installation that drips water into a shallow pool is a simple and soothing audio-visual feature of the courtyard. From the entrance, the display gallery covers the areas in front and to the left of the void, while the back and right house the kitchen and living room respectively. A staircase in front of the courtyard leads to more gallery space and an office on the second floor, while a staircase near the dining room leads to the living room and bedrooms. More offices and storage occupy the third floor.

Below left Objects are elegantly displayed in an open vitrine and on a single slab of thick timber at the end of the main gallery. Above, lights and air-conditioning units are hidden behind a simple structure covered with white fabric.

Right The display of objects extends to the galleries on the upper floors. The various stools and chairs on sale also allow visitors to sit and contemplate.

Below right Symmetry and balance characterize the façade. The large front doors, flanked by light fixtures, confer a sense of entry. Above the doors, an unusual wood screen filters light into the gallery.

Left This close-up of the canti-levered staircase between the second and third floors shows how the wall and steps have been plastered to a smooth finish but the color has been deliberately left uneven to contrast with the smooth brown wood on the parquet floor and table.

Above At the heart of the gallery house, the courtyard void brings light and air into the surrounding spaces. Water trickles down an installation composed of stone-like brass and copper objects affixed to horizontal brass rods to a swallow pool of water at the bottom. The element of ornamen-tation and the soothing sounds of water add visual and kinetic inter-est to the space. Folding wood-framed doors open to the dining room, another visual feast.

Right Set between two brick boxes, the protruding entrance bay of the house is clad in stones painted white to distinguish it from the rest of the structure. Vertical wood-framed windows inserted in the brick walls on each side of the entrance, on all three levels, add symmetry to the fa-çade. Concrete canopies shade the windows from the tropical sun.

Above left to right Juxtaposition is the hallmark of the interior of the gallery house: well-chosen, beautiful, man-made objects are placed against clean, tasteful, and contemporary backdrops to produce a sanctuary for the senses. Terracotta pots, water shimmering down a blind-like installation, sculptural plants in a simple vase, and a painted glass screen add color, texture—and sophistication—to the gallery.

Right The section view reveals the compact design of the multi-functional gallery house. Set on the entire buildable area—220 square meters—of the 335-square meter site, the structure extends all the way to the site lines on three sides.

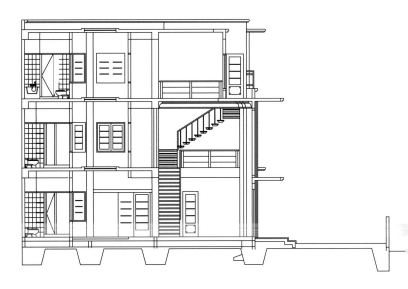

Opposite Wood-framed lights placed flush to the ceiling in the double-height entrance foyer give the impression of skylights cut into the ceiling. The modern chandelier is simply a circular band of tempered steel.

Above left A narrow corridor on the second floor, flanked by the void of the entrance foyer on one side and the void of the courtyard on the other, bridges the two sides of the gallery.

Above Another section view of the gallery house.

Below The bedrooms in the house, like this one, are minimalist cocoons lit by the tall windows on the façade. Simple hand-dyed linens dress the beds. Translucent glass panels form the walls of the wardrobe behind the headboard.

ab house

BUKIT DAGO, BANDUNG

ARCHITECT BASKORO TEDJO
BASKORO TEDJO AND ASSOCIATES

The design for this medium-sized site on the steeply sloping terrain of Dago Pakar Hill in North Bandung, was selected from nineteen entries submitted by the instructors and students of the Faculty of Architecture, Bandung Institute of Technology, in a special competition. Several factors had to be considered in designing a house for the site, especially the topography, slant of the slope, soil, and ground water content, as well as the needs of the client. What set architect Baskoro Tedjo's design apart from the other entries was his placement of the house twelve meters from the road rather than on the official setback line and his generous use of multiple layers of glass and steel grids to allow enviable views of the picturesque countryside.

The house is composed of two vertically staggered volumes, one slightly larger than the other. To best capitalize on its hillside location, the architect opted to place the volumes side by side rather than one in front of the other as in conventional split-level houses, an arrangement that allows the spaces on all levels to share the same views of the valley through the houses's expansive windows. The

main volume, propped up on stilts at the lower end of the site, is connected to the road level by a bridge placed at the left (south) of the site. The two volumes are woven together by means of a set of stairs, starting from outside the house, that link the levels between and within. The result is a series of spaces that visually connect with one another, and views to the outside that are balanced by views within the house.

Light and shade, visibility from the outside, views to the valley in the front (north) of the site, and airflow were of particular concern in the massing of the house. A simple terracotta hip roof helps to shelter the house from direct sunlight, particularly during the middle of the day, and the placement of the main structure away from the roadside also provides ample space for the fluid movement of air through the volumes. The platforms of the house, extending out towards the slope, protect the interior from intrusive views from the outside, at the same time allowing for the optimization of views to the outside.

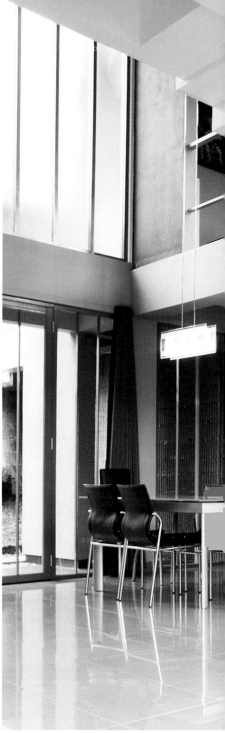

Left Different floor levels and partitions, such as the concrete wall screening the master bedroom, viewed from the study below, and the tall window walls create a multitude of vistas in the atrium-like interior.

Above A profound sense of asymmetrical balance in the arrangement of architectural elements and furniture underlines the overall openess and emphasis on natural light in the AB House. A stunning red chair, a red tribal mask, and a predominantly red contemporary painting offer some relief from the severity of the black and white palette.

Right In the first floor plan (left), the living room, the retracted dining room, and one of the bedrooms occupy the main volume, while another bedroom and the service areas take up the smaller, secondary space. In the second floor plan (right), the master bedroom, with its pentagonal bathtub, occupies most of the right-hand side of the main volume, while the study occupies the secondary volume. Steps lead to the bedroom from the entrance foyer in the middle of the house, between the void and the study.

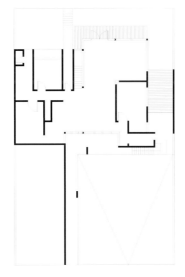

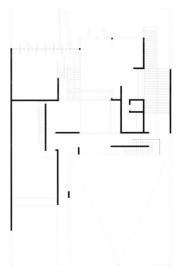

The volumes of the house are arranged around two circulation paths that connect the spaces both horizontally and vertically, the main path cutting through the two volumes, the second running between the sunken plaza at the back of the house. The main volume accommodates the living and dining rooms and a bedroom on the first floor, and the master bedroom on the second. The secondary volume houses a bedroom plus service areas on the first floor and the entrance foyer and study on the second.

There are two entrances to the house: visitors generally descend the exterior stairs to the lower level, but the house can also be entered via the upper level of the main volume. From the entrance foyer, visitors descend via a staircase to the living room below, which is set on a raised platform overlooking splendid views of the valley. The dining space, retracted behind the living room, also enjoys vistas, as does the bedroom next to the dining room facing east.

The master bedroom on the second floor of the main volume occupies the entire open space except for a study. A whirlpool bathtub placed in the corner of the bedroom allows the owners to enjoy the scenery as they bathe.

Above From the entrance foyer of the house, another set of steps, covered in striking dark granite, leads to the semi-enclosed master bedroom half a story above. Paintings by local artists adorn the walls throughout the house.

Above right The barrier between bedroom and bathroom is broken down in the master bedroom. Tall window walls allow unimpeded views of the Dago Valley from both the massive bed and the black granite-enclosed whirlpool.

Below right A small balcony cantilevered outside the study room is a good place for a refreshing break from work.

jane house

When planning this dwelling for a young couple with contrasting personalities and interests, the architect decided to reflect their dual natures in the façades of the house. The front façade basically expresses the introverted nature of the female owner. While the façade appears initially to be transparent and vulnerable to visual intrusion because of its wall of tall, thin, steel rods, the ground behind the fence is raised on a slant towards the front wall of the house, giving the impression that the house is tucked into the ground, protected from the outside world. In contrast, the rear of the house opens out to a swimming pool, the focal point of social activities, thus expressing the extroverted nature of the male owner. In essence, the house is faceless: the front elevation is hidden behind a slanted mound, while the back elevation is pitted against the high wall of the adjacent house. The orientation of the house echoes the rectangular site. Its structure fills the left half of the site, while the right half comprises a sparse garden.

CILANDAK, JAKARTA

ARCHITECT ANDRA MATIN
ANDRA MATIN ARCHITECT

Left above and below A thick transparent glass wall protects the open interior on the ground level. Although the front and the back of the house are conceptually divided from each other by a narrow circulation sliver in the middle of the house, spatially the areas of the house blend together. Once inside the house, visitors have immediate visual access to the dining area and pool beyond.

Below On an island in the center of the kitchen, a gray granite counter top, black cabinets, and a stainless steel hob and hood harmonize both materially and structurally with the rest of the house.

Right The side elevation (above) shows the house protected by a mound of grass in the front, and the yard at the back. The front elevation (below) indicates the introverted façade shielded by the pitched roof.

In plan, the house is composed of two rectangles sandwiching a smaller rectangular core, which contains a skylight-covered staircase leading to the second floor. Through the stairwell, the skylight brings light into both floors of the house. Placed back to back on the longitudinal site, the single-story rectangle in the front of the house comprises the garage, the entrance foyer, a television/games room, and a study. Its roof slants upwards towards the back of the house to accommodate the double-height living levels. The first floor is dominated by a long, open-plan living and dining area, which opens out to the swimming pool by means of sliding glass doors and to views of the garden through wood-framed windows. The spareness of the garden is highlighted by a single old frangipani tree.

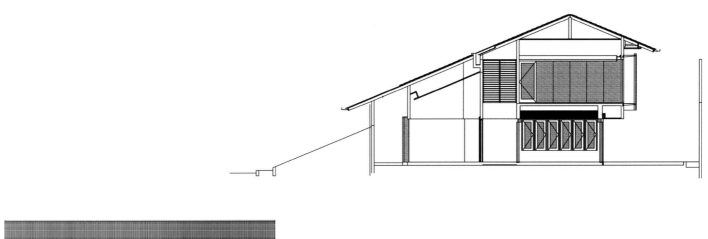

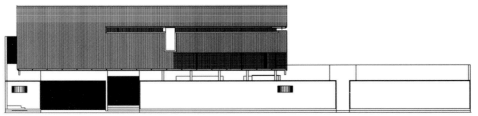

Above A graceful curving Arco lamp stands guard over the reproduction Barcelona day bed in the the minimalist living room. Behind it, within the circulation sliver dividing the front and back of the house, a concrete staircase covered with central wood treads leads to the second floor.

Right The living area, which is flooded with light on two sides, ends with a set of large timber-framed windows placed above a marble-clad ledge, on top of which decorative items can be placed. Under the ledge is a low cabinet for the storage of small items or books and magazines.

Wooden blinds harmonize perfectly with the dark-stained horizontal slats on the storage cupboards at the end of the living area. The broad marble shelf is an ideal place for displaying flowers, paintings, photographs, books, and other memorabilia.

A skylight placed along one side of the circulation sliver brings light into the narrow space. The combination of exposed painted plaster and the central passage of wood on the stairs and railings mirrors the materials used in the skylight area above.

Beneath the stairs, a bed of pebbles becomes a clever spatial device for separating the staircase from the rest of the space without physically blocking it off. The mix of concrete, wood, pebbles, and tiles demonstrates the subtle use of colors and textures in the house.

The bedrooms on the second floor also face the pool but are given privacy from the adjoining property by a linear screen of wood. Two projections jut out from the main volume on the upper level above the glass-clad lower floor, sheltering the lower floor from the elements but also creating a feeling of intimacy at the back of the house. The first is an extension of the master bedroom, the other projects from one of the children's bathrooms.

Incorporating famed designer Mies van der Rohe's concept of indoors–outdoors, the minimalist living/dining area merges seamlessly with the pool running alongside the length of the house, sandwiched between the structure and the old rustic brick wall bordering the site. A water spout emerging from a concrete column at one end of the pool circulates water in the pool, which overflows on all sides, then comes back into the pool. Lights installed in the plastered cement slabs of the narrow path between the pool and the brick wall, highlight both the path and the wall. In an alcove at the far end of the pool is a changing room and a separate toilet. The opposite end of the pool opens to the expansive lawn with its sole frangipani.

While the layouts of the front and back rectangles appear to further reflect the dual natures of the owners— the front occupied by fixed, enclosed spaces, the back by versatile, open spaces—the architect has introduced architectural devices that allow tremendous flexibility in the arrangement of both rectangles. Sliding walls transform the configuration of the television/games room and study vis-à-vis the living room. Instead of a simple door, a folding wall is installed to separate the entrance foyer from the open living and dining space beyond, allowing the house to have two different and even contrasting personalities.

Opposite above The linearity of the pool area at the back is emphasized by the use of horizontal wood slats on the upper level, the long rustic brick wall, and the coarse unpainted plastered cement paving blocks.

Above A curved concrete wall leads towards the entrance, at the same time acting as a retaining wall for the protective grass mound in front of the house.

Left The top of the roof rests high above the axis of the middle of the back volume, its girders jutting out the sides. Sloping towards the front of the house, the roof cantilevers over the birm resting on a frame of concrete erected as a screen wall behind the retaining wall of the mound.

Left Window screens constructed of pieces of bamboo bring the earthy textures of the sunken garden into the house, creating a tactile threshold between the inside and out.

Right "Informal grandeur" sums up the double-height gallery-cum-living area. Traditional Chinese-crafted red doors on the left and the cast concrete stairs leading to the bedroom level on the right illustrate the calculated blending of scalar elements.

PURI INDAH, JAKARTA

ARCHITECT ALBERTUS WANG
SW1M-CAU

t house

In this remarkable transformation of an existing structure, architect Albertus Wang has conquered the many design shortcomings of the previous building, as well as the limitations of a longitudinal site walled in on three sides, to produce a modern residence distinguished by its dynamic geometric forms, linear connectivity, and illusions of space. The result is a sophisticated and elegant dwelling, a visual and spatial delight that stands in marked contrast to the heavily ornated façades of most of its neighbors in this élite residential enclave in West Jakarta.

From the street, the structure appears as a large white and gray box articulated with three abstract masses, the middle one faced with horizontally raked cement and the

two flanking it painted white and pierced with narrow openings. A simple black linear balustrade, a colorful red door, a waterfall, and lotus ponds provide contrast to the clean, modern, and simple lines of the exterior.

The three masses of the house run longitudinally along the length of the site, ending with a fourth, transverse volume at the back. The main organizing element—located in the first, central mass—is a double-height gallery/living space that connects the other three volumes and provides the main horizontal circulation. From this tall, open box extend three staircases connecting the three levels of the house. The second mass, located to the left of the central, open box, contains a bedroom on the first floor, above the garage, and two more bedrooms with a shared bathroom on the third floor. The third mass, on the opposite side of the house, is occupied by a music room on the first floor, an informal living room on the second, and a library on the third. At the back of the house, the fourth mass houses the main living room, kitchen, maid's quarters, and other

service areas on the first floor, the dining room and pantry on the second, and the master bedroom on the third.

The interior of the house is a fusion of innovative devices for space expansion, contemporary materials, and intriguing design ideas. Although the house is undoubtedly introverted, its exterior shell making full use of the site right up to the boundary walls, it is nevertheless punctuated with "pockets" of space along the periphery—judicious cutaways of the original walls—that not only let in light and air but also visually expand the first-floor living spaces outward, through picture glass doors, to the walls bordering the lot. Such pockets, including a breakfast alcove adjacent to the kitchen, a sand garden, and a "pine forest," also relieve the introversion of the house and encourage various family-oriented activities and interests.

While highly crafted detailing throughout the house highlights the spaces within, it is the entranceway to the house that is most telling. The entrance "procession" advances through a complex sequence of stepping stones,

Left Raked cement walls and broad glass windows bring the mood of the "pine forest" garden at the rear of the site into the main living space, at the same time carrying through the architectural themes of the house: geometric forms, linear connectivity, and illusions of space.

Above An eclectic mix of materials at the entry alcove—raked cement, red lacquered wood, and natural slate—blend tradition with modernity, offering a subtle statement on the nature of dwelling in the modern world.

Right A view from the stepped entry sequence of the three parallel volumes of the house, the central one finished in handcrafted raked cement, the other two painted white. The custom-made steel handrail echoes the house's linear detailing.

across a waterfall and terraced pools, ending at a tucked-in sliver between the central scraped concrete box and the frame of the library volume. While the door is bright red, it is discreetly concealed, hinting at a contradiction between hesitation and pride. In fact, the entire house is an expression of dualities: heavy and light, light and dark, modern and traditional, spacious and intimate, restricted and liberated. These represent the house's socio-cultural context as well as the story behind its creation. The design process had to deal with the very real problems of the existing structure: illogical size, scale, punctuation, connection, location, and orientation, exemplified by the cantilevered bedroom placed too low over the main staircase and poorly placed columns and walls. Some irreversible problem areas, which display unorthodox treatments and unexpected details, have even been preserved as a part of the history of the house and add to its overall interest.

Opposite An astute marriage of hand-worked finishes, delicate stair details, and the modulation of light within the double-height gallery/living room creates a warm yet modern interior. The specially made handrail of the upper floor balcony is extended to create a floating architectural composition with a musical quality. The built-in pantry and glass-partitioned staircase leading to the lower level are visible in the rear.

Above The dualities of heavy and light and light and dark are evident in the dining room where a cool concrete floor—an extension of the cement walls of the exterior garden—meets a dark wood ceiling and where white walls and dining chairs meet dark tables. Dramatic transformations in the quality of light entering the house through-out the day add to the ambience. An arrangement of twigs softens the staircase partition.

Above Balanced with a simple wood table and earthy collectibles, a comfortable leather-upholstered sofa positioned for viewing the flat-screen television on the ledge next to the rear wall of the living area, makes a thoroughly modern statement.

Left Formal and informal are blended in the kitchen and the adjoining outdoor breakfast patio, accessed through folding wood-framed doors. Playful bar stools are a perfect foil to an almost life-size bronze sculpture by artist Teguh Ostenrik.

Above A custom-built media wall in the family music room on the first floor provides ample yet readily accessible storage space.

Right from left The first, second, and third floor plans show the stepped entry sequence, vertical circulation, double-height volumes and "carved" pocket gardens in this house, which is bounded on three sides by high property walls. Some elements of the plan are left over from the pre-existing structural shell.

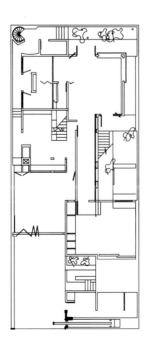
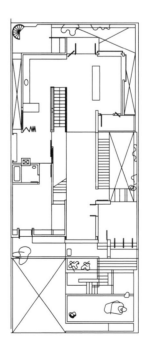
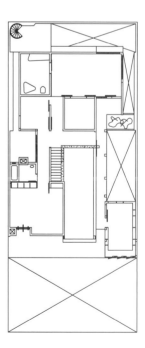

setiadharma house

setiadharma house

Left A dark-stained pergola projecting from a bold wood-clad box leads to the garage door but also diffuses sunlight and protects visitors from rain. The steps between the pillars take visitors along a short glass passage to the entrance. The wood-clad box houses a study on the first level and a bedroom on the second.

Right A striking double-height wood screen connects the two main volumes of the house. The slats on the lower part are spaced further apart to allow air to flow into the inner courtyard behind, while the upper half is more tightly slatted to moderate light entering the gallery on the second floor.

PONDOK INDAH, JAKARTA

ARCHITECT KUSUMA AGUSTIANTO
GRAHACIPTA HADIPRANA

Designed for an extremely busy businessman who, at the end of a long, hectic day, likes to return to an oasis of calm where he can enjoy his collection of art and other pleasures of life, this house is located in a highly private and tranquil neighborhood, yet is not too far from the central business district of metropolitan Jakarta.

The house is set above street level, and both its elevation and distance from the front of the lot contribute to its serenity. Taking into consideration his client's lifestyle and need for privacy, architect Kusuma Agustianto delved into the way art is made in order to gain inspiration for his design. While great attention has been placed on the division of public and private areas, circulation, efficiency, and the functional relationship between and among spaces,

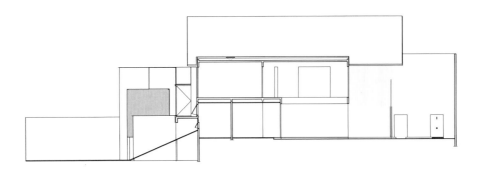

Left above and center The reflections from the pools in the courtyard and the sounds of the water weave an intimate spell over the house. The breakfast room and living room, at right angles to each other, open out to the courtyard.

Below left Section view.

Below right Sandwiched between the central courtyard and the swimming pool at the back of the house, the living room enjoys the benefits of both.

Pages 214–15 Placed in the very center of the courtyard, the prosperity pool, shaped in the form of the infinity symbol or the number eight, rises from the lower rectangular pool. Water flows from the upper to the lower pool. Four footstool palms provide shade and color to the austere courtyard.

the architect also offers an artistic solution to the pragmatic concerns of everyday living by juxtaposing contrasting elements: light versus dark, high versus low, open versus closed, transparent versus massive, liquid versus solid.

The house is made up of five volumes: three laid out across the width of the lot in front—two main volumes separated by a central volume—and two flanking the main volumes at right angles at the back. Protruding from the front of the house, the two largest volumes dominate the façade. One, faced with dark-stained *ulin* wood, forms a massive box that demarcates the entrance. A wooden gateway under the box leads to the underground garage. Between the front of the box and the garage gate, steps running across the front of the house lead to the entrance foyer, set within the second box, which is painted white. Beyond the entrance foyer, steps lead visitors to the main level of the house, which is located on the second floor.

Between the two projecting volumes is a lower, lattice-clad structure that connects the front of the house to the central courtyard behind and the rooms leading off it.

The two structures at the back of the house, at right angles to the dominant "boxes" in front, flank a central courtyard accessed by either sliding or pivoting glass doors. At the far end of the courtyard, the thin structure of the staircase becomes a visually exciting sculptural element. A double-tiered pool, shaped in the form of the infinity symbol or the number eight, denoting "prosperity," dominates the courtyard. From this pool, water flows into another, lower rectangular pool following the form of the courtyard itself. Four footstool palm trees emerge from the corners of the lower main pool, providing some shade and a colorful touch to what is otherwise a relatively austere courtyard, while a border of grass also adds a softening touch. Together the pools form a cool, soft, fluid water

Left From the courtyard, different angles produce different views into the rooms. Behind the simple glass-topped breakfast table, the kitchen is hidden behind the counter of the pantry. The series of floor-pivoted painted aluminum doors in the breakfast room swing open towards the courtyard, bringing elements of nature into the house.

Center Entrance to the house is up a short flight of steps located just behind the timber-framed structure on the front façade.

Right Low sloping stairs in this corridor ascend from the entrance foyer directly to the study and breakfast room. The corridor also connects the two main volumes of the house.

element at the heart of the house, while the open courtyard allows air and light to enter. A simple gable roof covers the U-shaped areas surrounding the courtyard, before meeting with the two main volumes at the front. Beyond the living room bordering one side of the courtyard, the entire space at the back of the house is an open area that includes a garden and swimming pool.

Located in the first dark volume on the left of the house is a study, pantry, breakfast area, and dining room on the first story and a bedroom and another study on the second story. The kitchen, laundry, and the maids' bedrooms are also located in this left-hand volume. Arranged within the second, white volume is a guest room and service areas such as toilets. Beyond these, and dominating the white volume, is the master bedroom, which opens to a terrace beside the swimming pool at the back of the site. The level of the front and back parts of this section differ by half a

Below A border of lush but low-maintenance water plants is used to soften the edge of the swimming pool near the wall at the back of the site. The pool extends the length of the master bedroom and living room combined—two-thirds the width of the site—forming a cool oasis in a high-density urban area. An extension from the master bedroom forms an outdoor terrace. A low wooden bench along the side of the living room is a handy seat for viewing the pool.

Bottom From the back yard of the house, the three volumes are clearly visible. While the master bedroom and living room correspond to the length of the swimming pool, the third volume, accommodating the formal dining room, opens to a grass yard.

Above right A sliding wooden door separates the breakfast area from the formal dining room. The breakfast area is connected to the pantry through an opening cut between the rooms. While the casual breakfast room is equipped with a modern steel frame glass top table and modern versions of Arne Jacobsen's Model 3107 chair, the adjoining formal dining room is furnished with heavier, more stately wood furniture.

Below right The first floor plan of the house shows the main rooms in relation to the central courtyard and prosperity pools and to the swimming pool against the boundary wall at the back.

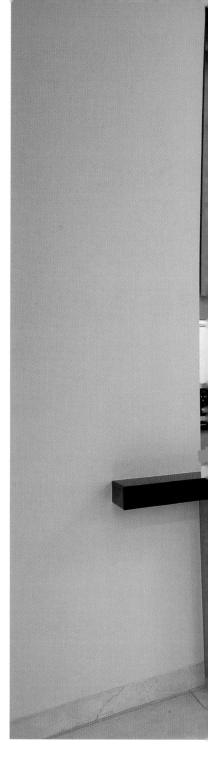

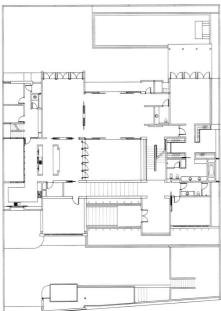

story. Above the master bedroom, on the second floor, is another bedroom and a music room. The landing mid-level between the first and second levels opens out to a terrace. Another simple gable roof structure covers this section of the house.

The rooms towards the back of the house are able to enjoy views of the open space: the formal dining room faces the garden, while the living room and the master bedroom both face the swimming pool. But the most commanding views from the central courtyard and the front of the house and the garden in the back, can be seen from the living room on the first floor and the gallery on the second floor, undoubtedly the most prominent spaces in the house.

edi & hetty home

Left The house is basically composed of two open boxes stacked one on top of the other and protected by a protruding corrugated metal roof and a glass wall affixed to a steel frame. Timber-framed glass doors open to the garden.

Above A tall table and a pair of bar chairs signal the entrance foyer, which spills into the open-plan living/dining area. The door on the left leads to the garage, while the staircase on the right goes up to the second floor.

The location of the Edi and Hetty Home in the Ragunan area of South Jakarta was a distinct challenge to architect Adi Purnomo. Houses in the Ragunan area are required to be aligned to a ten-meter building recess line regardless of the depth of the lot. While most plots in the neighborhood used to be over 1000 square meters, today many, if not most, have been split into smaller parcels of land and sold off. The lot on which this house stands has a depth of only around fifteen meters. Given the regulation ten-meter recess line, the buildable area was effectively reduced to a mere five meters from front to back.

The architect has chosen to turn this "loss" into an advantage by opting for a design based on the traditional *rumah panggung* (platform house), whereby the first floor of the house, which ranges across almost the entire width of the lot, is reserved for "public" or "communal" spaces, while the second is designated private space. In this way, the design maximizes the available buildable area.

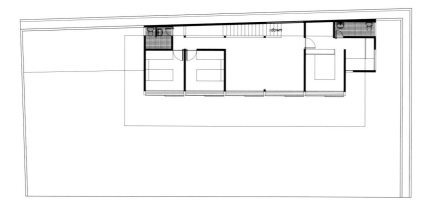

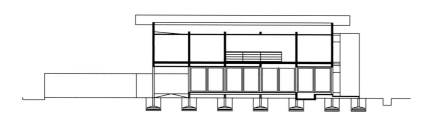

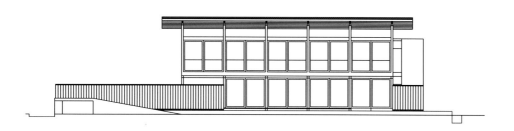

Above left The second floor plan (top), section view (middle), and back elevation (below) all show the simplicity of the house's design.

Left and above A row of white built-in cabinets forms a wall screening the staircase from the open-plan living and dining areas on the first floor. The wooden floor extends out to the edge of the verandah, visually expanding the size of the space. The kitchen, placed behind the dining area, is the only physically closed-in room. The colors in the painting in the "foyer" are picked up in the simple modern furniture and accessories.

He has also treated the area in front of the house as a natural external "atrium" into which the spaces on both stories of the house extend. Vegetation is allowed to grow wild along the fence, emphasizing the boundaries of the site and demarcating the edge of this external "void."

Because the house faces south, the architect was able to create a steel-framed rectangular box with a transparent screen façade stretching the entire length of the upper floor of the house. Cantilevered over a series of steel columns that are retracted from the edge of the verandah below, the spaces on this second floor, encased within the "floating" glass box, extend to the natural external "atrium" created by the ten-meter recess line. The columns appear to pierce the box from underneath, except for a gap where a set of large wood-framed glass doors open to the verandah. Otherwise, the construction creates five equal-sized bays

which correspond to the way in which the internal spaces are organized. A corrugated iron roof is cantilevered over the floating glass box, providing shade and preventing rainfall from entering the house, at the same time enhancing the fusion between the inside and outside spaces.

The notion of inside–outside is heightened by the continuous wooden flooring that extends from the main space of the first floor, though the four sets of swinging doors, and into the garden in front of the house. This also creates the illusion that the house is bigger than it really is.

The entrance to the house, on the left of the site, is concealed by a wooden picket fence. A horizontally slatted wooden screen adjacent to the first set of doors shields views to the garage. Once inside the house, the longitudinal wood-floored open space on the first floor ends with the dining area and kitchen at the far end.

Access to the rooms on the second floor is via a wood-lined set of stairs hidden behind a slender row of white-painted cabinets. On the upper floor, the first two bays accommodate the two children's bedrooms. The master bedroom is placed in the fifth bay, and extends out to a small extension that slightly protrudes from the main floating box. Occupying two bays between the children's bedrooms and the master bedroom is the family living room. Paralleling the cabinets below, another set of cabinets on the second floor shields the staircase and its simple steel balustrade. A similar balustrade provides protection in front of the glass windows, while the wooden ceiling above the staircase echoes the material used on the stairs and on the floor below.

Above far left The family room commands views of the garden below through the continuous glass walls covering the entire façade of the second floor. Waist-high white metal railings placed inside the glass provide security.

Above left and left The staircase, lined in wood, leads directly to the living room on the second floor. From here, a corridor goes to the children's bedrooms. The open white metal railing makes the corridor feel more spacious, while the gray-toned ceramic floors and pale green furnishings add light-ness and brightness.

Above The master bedroom also overlooks the garden in front through the glass wall opening which brings plenty of light into the room. Bright red hanging heli-conias and colorful bedding con-trast well with the pale walls and curtains.

Right Large wood-framed glass swinging doors allow generous access to the verndah and garden. The continuous flooring expands the space. A trim of pebbles forms the drip line for the overhanging corrugated metal roof.

Left The entrance to the house is shielded by a wall clad in slate within the wood-slatted box that extends out to the fence line. On the right, a white limestone wall greets visitors to the house.

Right The façade of the house is a composition of forms—volumes protruding out of or layered over the main structure—textures, and colors. A sturdy metal gate covered in thick wood planks rolls in and out of the wood-slatted box.

tall house

NORTH JAKARTA

ARCHITECT AHMAD DJUHARA
DJUHARA+DJHUARA

An increasingly important factor in the design of modern houses in Indonesia is security. Social turbulence brought about by imbalances in the distribution of wealth, increasing polarization of society, and marginalization of the poor, has led to a desire among Indonesia's middle and upper middle classes for houses where people can retreat and have protection from current social and urban realities.

From the street, the three-story house, located in a newly developed area in North Jakarta, appears vast and inscrutable. The façade is a composition of screens and planes that form a protective barrier against the outside. To further "protect" the house from its surroundings, the architect has chosen to elevate it rather than simply orientate it inwards. A basement level has therefore been constructed at street level, raising the living area of the house a full story above ground. In addition, the clients' brief called for an extraordinary ceiling height of 4.5 meters on both the second and third floors, making the house stand even taller and appear even more forbidding.

Completely filling its 750-square meter site, the house is composed of three longitudinal north–south masses. On the façade, the central mass is distinguished from the two white masses flanking it by its tall hip roof, its subtle Bali gold color and, above all, the wood-slatted box that extends to the fence line, functioning as a barrier for the steps leading to the entrance. To the left of the central mass, tall stepped terracing provides a transition from the street to the second level. In the middle of the terraces, large yellow bamboo plants fence the street, forming a further barrier to the white, flat-roofed volume behind. The white volume on the right is shielded from view by the gate leading to the garage.

Above left The front elevation.

Above, left, and right High ceilings, expansive travertine flooring, a glass-encased staircase, a controlled palette, and spare modernist furniture inject a Zen feel in the open-plan living and dining areas, which are flooded with light from the pivoting wood-framed glass doors opening out to the swimming pool at the far corner of the site. The combined living space gives the occupants room to breathe and contemplate textures and tones. The dining area is separated from a kitchenette at the far end by a waist-high counter concealing the barest of kitchen essentials: a small microwave and a double-door refrigerator, both in sleek metallic finishes, contributing to the minimalist hitech look. A pair of lamps suspended from the ceiling mark the position of the dining table. A couple of bright red single-seaters in the living area add a splash of color to the largely monochromatic color scheme.

The basement, which occupies the longitudinal central and right-hand masses on the first (ground) level of the house, contains parking for three cars in the front half, flanked by staircases leading to the second floor, and servants' quarters at the back, also linked to the upstairs.

After climbing the steps within the wood-slatted box to the second floor entrance porch, visitors enter a guest living room through a set of doors to the right. Beyond the entrance and the guest living room, the central mass houses the dining room, which flows seamlessly into a spacious living room on the left of the site set between two large, unenclosed spaces. These voids are filled with gardens and a pool, accessed from both dining and living areas through wood-framed pivoting doors. The kitchen is located at the far back, while a bathroom and guest room are placed between two lightwells in the right-hand mass. The main focus of the second floor, however, is decidedly on the left where the two gardens and pool provide spatial continuity to the elevated ground plane. Sunlight animates the living and dining areas, entering through the glass doors, while the smaller lightwells on the right also bring light into the house and allow plenty of cross-ventilation.

The third level is reached via a steep, double-split staircase protected by a thick glass railing. Slightly cantilevered above the staircase and adjacent lightwell is a blue box housing an enclosed family room. Here, once again, the architect plays with the spatial relationship and scales of the prominent blue volume vis-à-vis the spaces beneath it, especially as can be seen from the staircase landing. From a glass desk in the box placed against the opening facing the lightwell, one can experience the interplay of volumes within volumes and spaces.

Surrounding the central family room are four bedrooms: the master bedroom with adjoining bathroom and walk-in closet to the north, two bedrooms on the left above the living room, and another in front above the entrance porch. Panels of light-colored timber cover the walls of the master bedroom, while a darker reddish tone of timber is used for the floors, and an even darker coffee tone for the wooden furniture. The use of timber in the bedrooms creates a subtle composition of colors and provides tremendous warmth in contrast to the relatively cold materials and neutral colors employed in the more public areas of the house.

Left The longitudinal dining area, with the kitchenette at one end and a washroom to the side, is ideal for entertaining. A large white wall makes a perfect backdrop for displaying modern art.

Above The entrance to the house is encased within a wood-slatted structure that protects it visually and, to a certain extent, also physically and yet allows light and air to pass through.

Right The longitudinal second floor plan (left) shows the living area on the left sandwiched between the pool and front garden, and the dining area, kitchenette, and (at the far end) the kitchen in the middle volume. The guest living room, bathroom, and guest bedroom range to the right. On the third floor (right), four bedrooms surround the family room.

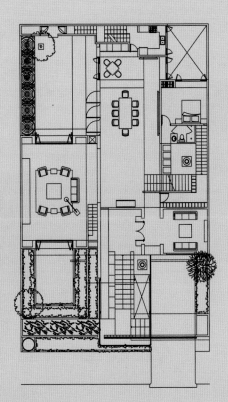
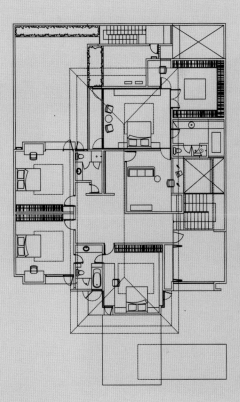

Left A sculptural two-tiered staircase composed of concrete, wood, stainless steel, and glass visibly ascends over a bed of gravel from the second to the third floor.

Right In the master bedroom, a bold black headboard with protruding side tables conceals electronic gadgets. The glowing wood veneer wall behind, lit by concealed ceiling lights, adds drama to the room. The dark tones of the bed are repeated in the chairs, cushions, and flooring.

Below left and right The family room, encased in blue walls, adjoins the study which overlooks the double-height staircase through a large glass opening. The study table has been specially constructed of thick laminated glass in keeping with the overall transparency of the house.

Adi Purnomo

Born in Yogjakarta in 1968, Adi Purnomo studied architecture at Gadjah Mada University in his home town. After working for Pacific Adhika Internusa in Jakarta and DP Architects in Singapore in the 1990s, he started his own architectural studio in 2000. He received the Association of Indonesian Architects (Ikatan Arsitek Indonesia—IAI) Award for Residential Architecture in 2002. He is an active member of the Forum of Young Indonesian Architects (Arsitek Muda Indonesia—AMI), and has participated in their exhibitions held in various cities around Java and also in The Hague, The Netherlands. His works have appeared in various publications locally as well as internationally, and were also included in an exhibition with the Van Allen Institute in New York. Recently, he has become a popular critic/reviewer and guest lecturer at several universities in Jakarta.

Studioarsitektur

Jl. Bangka VIII C No. 23
Jakarta 12730

Tel: (6221) 7199839/7199841
E-mail: dentingsepi@yahoo.com

Ahmad Djuhara

Ahmad Djuhara, born in Jakarta in 1966, graduated from Parahyangan Catholic University, Bandung, in 1991. From 1992 he worked as a project architect in Pacific Adhika Indonesia (1992–8) and as an architect with J. Budiman Architects (1999–2001). He established his own firm, Ahmad Djuhara, in 2001, but since 2004 has been in partnership with his wife Wendy in the firm djuhara+djuhara. His designs have received several awards and mentions. With his wife, he has also received a number of awards, including first place for the Megalopolis Gallery House, Tarumanegara University, Jakarta, in 1997, and honorable mention in the JakArt@ 2001 Jakarta Art Festival's competition for an art center. The design for the Rawa Buaya bus station, developed with Nataneka (Jeffrey Sandi, Sukendro Sukendar, and Wendy Djuhara), won third place in a competition held by the Jakarta Chapter of the IAI and the Bureau for Transportation of Jakarta. Most recently, the design for the Museum Wayang extension won first place in a competition held by IAI Jakarta and the Bureau for Culture and Museums of Jakarta, in 2004. He is an active member of the Forum of Young Indonesian Architects (Arsitek Muda Indonesia—AMI).

djuhara+djuhara

Jl. Galunggung 764
Bukit Nusa Indah
Ciputat 15414

Tel/Fax: (6221) 74702083
E-mail: djuhara@dnet.net.id

Albertus Wang

Albertus Wang was born in Indonesia, but has since divided his time between Italy, USA, and Indonesia. He received a Bachelor of Design in Architecture with High Honors from the University of Florida and a Master of Architecture from Harvard. He has also completed a program at the Vicenza Institute of Architecture in Italy. He has received several awards and recognitions for his outstanding scholastic contribution in the US and elsewhere, including from the American Institute of Architects and American Architectural Foundation. Wang's work includes winning entries for the Foshan International Urban Competition under Sanders Wang MacLeod International Consortium for Architecture and Urbanism (SWiM-CAU); the Milwaukee International Urban Design Competition, the Head-start Program, and the Kawachi-Mura prefabricated modular housing system. His designs have appeared in Harvard and Florida University publications and international magazines. He has taught at several architecture schools in the US and elsewhere. He continues to explore the architecture and urbanism of Asian cities.

SWiM-CAU

1633 NW 14th Avenue
Gainesville
Florida 32605

Tel: (632) 352-3718001
Fax: (632) 352-3710043
E-mail: info@swimcau.com;
albertus@landsbetween.com
Website: www.swimcau.com

Andra Matin

Isandra (Andra) Matin, the Principal of Andra Matin Architect, was born in Bandung in 1962, and received his formal training in architecture at the Parahyangan Catholic University, Bandung. In 1999, he received the IAI Award (for a commercial building) for the LeBoYe graphic design office in Jakarta, and an honorable mention for his entry in a competition for an art gallery, juried by Antoine Predock, in 2001. Another of his striking buildings, the Gedung Dua8, received an IAI Award citation in 2002. In 2004, he was named winner of the Mowilex Award (for residential exteriors). Andra became a member of the master jury of the Pertubuhan Arkitek Malaysia Award in 2004. He has also been a guest lecturer at the University of Indonesia and at the Pertubuhan Arkitek Malaysia in Kuala Lumpur (2003), and Kuching, Sarawak (2004). He is a founding member of the Forum of Young Indonesian Architects (Arsitek Muda Indonesia—AMI), and remains an active and influential member.

Andra Matin Architect

Jl. Manyar 111 blok O-3 kav. 30
Sektor 1, Bintaro Jaya
Jakarta 12330

Tel: (6221) 7353338/73692258
Fax: (6221) 7352165
E-mail: andra168@cbn.net.id

Antony Liu

Antony Budiwihardja was born in Jakarta in 1967. He studied architecture at Tarumanegara University, Jakarta, graduating in 1991. He started his career as an architect at Pakar Cipta Graha, Jakarta, before setting up his own architectural practice in Jakarta in 1996. Together with Ferry Ridwan, in 1999– 2000 he designed the Bale Resort, Nusa Dua, and the Oasis 1 & 2 in Bali, as well as a sports club in Cimanggis, West Java. Antony is currently working on a number of houses, clubs, lounges, and restaurants in Jakarta. He is an active member of the Forum of Young Indonesian Architects (Arsitek Muda Indonesia—AMI).

PT Dwitunggal Mandiri

Plaza Kebon Jeruk E11
Jl. Raya Pejuangan Kebon Jeruk
Jakarta Barat 11530

Tel: (6221) 5350319/5350325/
5350334
Fax: (6221) 5356268

Baskoro Tedjo

Upon graduating from Bandung Institute of Technology in 1982, Baskoro Tedjo, who was born in Semarang in 1956, took up an appointment as an assistant lecturer at his alma mater. He was appointed to the technical team preparing the Indonesian pavilion at the 1986 World Exposition in Vancouver, Canada, then on a Fullbright grant he continued his studies at the Poly University in New York (1987–9). On returning home, he continued to teach, but also worked at the Bandung office of the Atelier Enam architectural firm. Between 1995 and 1999, he pursued his doctorate at Osaka University on an OECF scholarship. He continued teaching and established his own firm, Baskoro Tedjo and Associates. He has received numerous awards for his designs, among them first place in a competition for a house at Dago Resort, Bandung (2001) and the Jakarta monorail station, as well as the IAI Award for his design of the Selasar Sunaryo. He was also selected to design the Sukarno monument in Blitar, East Java.

Baskoro Tedjo and Associates

Jl. Dederuk 25
Bandung

Tel/Fax: (632) 022-2506080
E-mail: hepta7@cbn.net.id

Budiman Hendropurnomo

Budiman Holan Hendropurnomo, IAI, FRAIA, was born in Malang, East Java, in 1954. He received his Bachelor of Architecture (Hons) from the University of Melbourne in 1981. After gaining early experience in the Netherlands and Australia, he joined Denton Corker Marshall in Melbourne, and in 1991 became a full partner of the international firm, focusing on tourism industry projects in Indonesia. Since the mid-1980s he has designed many award-winning hotels, entertainment and shopping centers, and apartments in Indonesia, including the Tugu Park Hotel in Malang, the Novotel Surabaya, the Maya Ubud Resort & Spa (winner of four awards, including the TTG Travel Awards 2002 for Best New Resort), the Ex – Entertainment Center in Plaza Indonesia Complex, Jakarta, and the Howard House and Prapanca Townhouses. He is currently working on the Manhattan Hotel, Jakarta, the Westin, Jakarta, the Marriott Nusa Dua, Bali, the Payangan Resort & Spa in Ubud, Bali, and the Boracay Island Resort & Spa in the Philippines.

Denton Corker Marshall Pty Ltd

PT Duta Cermat Mandiri
Wijaya Graha Puri Blok G-30
Jalan Wijaya II
Kebayoran Baru
Jakarta 12160

Tel: (6221) 7210210
Fax: (6221) 7202926
E-mail: dcm@indo.net.id
Webmail: http://www.dentoncorkermarshall.com

Cosmas Gozali

Cosmas D. Gozali studied at the Technische Universitats Wien. Vienna, Austria, where he received his Architek Diplom Ingeneur in 1992. On graduation, he worked as a junior designer at the ateliers of Karl Mang and Reinhard Geiselman, both in Vienna. In 1992, together with Judistira (Judi) Wanandi, he founded Architelier (PT Archindo Ciptakreatif), based in Jakarta. In 2002, the firm received an IAI Award for Rumah Ganesha, a small resort in Ubud, Bali, and the ICI Award for Rumah Origami, Bandung, and Rumah Opera, Jakarta.

Architelier (PT Archindo Ciptakreatif)

Jalan Raya Kebayoran Lama No. 1
Jakarta 11560

Tel: (6221) 5361179/5361180
Fax: (6221) 5356084
E-mail: cosmas@architelier.net;
cdgozali@singnet.com.sg
Website: www.architelier.net

Dicky Hendrasto

Dicky Hendrasto was born in Jakarta in 1965. In 1988, while still a student at the University of Indonesia, he won first place in the Architectural Student Association of Asia (ASASIA) Indonesia competition and represented Indonesia in the ASASIA Jamboree in Seoul, South Korea. After receiving his Bachelor of Architecture (Hons.) from the University of Indonesia in 1989, he joined Duta Cermat Mandiri/Denton Corker Marshall Jakarta. He became an associate of Denton Corker Marshall in 1996 and in 2004 was appointed Associate Director of Denton Corker Marshall Pty Ltd. His designs for EX Plaza and Maya Ubud have earned the company numerous architectural awards. He is a founding member of the Forum of Young Indonesian Architects (Arsitek Muda Indonesia—AMI).

Denton Corker Marshall Pty Ltd

PT Duta Cermat Mandiri
Wijaya Graha Puri Blok G-30
Jalan Wijaya II
Kebayoran Baru
Jakarta 12160

Tel: (6221) 7210210
Fax: (6221) 7202926
E-mail: dcm@indo.net.id
Webmail: http://www.dentoncorkermarshall.com

Faried Masdoeki

Ir. Muhamad Faried MS. Masdoeki was born in Singkep, Riau, in 1963. While studying at the Parahyangan Catholic University in Bandung, he designed a number of houses in Bandung. After graduating in 1988, he joined the Grahacipta Hadiprana architectural firm, and was immediately given the responsibility of architect-in-charge or principal architect of several residences, villas, apartments, hotels, and housing developments in Jakarta, Bogor, Semarang, Surabaya, and Bali. In 2003, he was appointed Managing/Operational Director of the firm.

Grahacipta Hadiprana

Jl. Pangeran Antasari No. 12
Cipete Selatan
Jakarta Selatan 12410

E-mail: gch@cbn.net.id
Website: www.grahaciptahadiprana.com

Ferry Ridwan

Born in Bandung in 1970, Ferry Ridwan studied architecture at Tarumanegara University in Jakarta, graduating in 1993. He initially worked as an architect at Pakar Cipta Graha, Jakarta, before joining Antony Liu at PT Dwitunggal Mandiri Jaya. In 1999–2000, he worked with Liu on the design of the Bale Resort, Nusa Dua, the Oasis 1 & 2 in Bali, and a sports club in Cimanggis, West Java. He is currently working on a few hotels in Bali, such as the Conrad extension and chapel and the Bale extension. He is also designing the Panorama Headquarters Tower, an eight-story office building in Jakarta, and a resort on Sentosa Island, Singapore. He has also given lectures at the Indonesian Architectural Association (IAI) Forum.

PT Dwitunggal Mandiri

Plaza Kebon Jeruk E11
Jl. Raya Pejuangan Kebon Jeruk
Jakarta Barat 11530

Tel: (6221) 5350319/5350325/5350334
Fax: (6221) 5356268

Irianto PH

Irianto Purnomo Hadi was born in Jakarta in 1961. After studying architecture at the Department of Architecture, University of Indonesia, Jakarta, he joined the architectural firms Armekon Reka Tantra (1989–90) and Pacific Adhika Internusa (1990–2003), both based in Jakarta. Currently, he is the Principal of Antara, his private practice established in 2001. Irianto has participated in several architectural competitions and won first place for his design for the Bank Exim Kemayoran, Jakarta (1991) and second place for the design of the Ford Foundation Headquarters, Jakarta (1992). He is a founding member of the Forum of Young Indonesian Architects, and has become the Vice President of the Jakarta Chapter of the Indonesian Institute of Architects.

Antara Design

Jl. Cibodas II No. 37 Puri Cinere
South Jakarta

Tel: (6221) 7541950

Jaya Ibrahim

Jaya Ibrahim spent the first ten years of his career in London as a design assistant to the internationally famous Anouska Hempel. In 1993, he returned to Indonesia and formed his own company, Jaya & Associates, which has become well known worldwide for its design concepts and attention to detail. Jaya's years in the West allowed him to view his own Indonesian culture afresh and to create designs that incorporate characteristics specific to each locale. He has been involved in many high-profile design projects in Indonesia, including the renovation of the Jakarta Town Hall, the Legian hotel in Bali, the expansion concept of the Indonesian National Museum, the Amanjiwo resort, the renovation of the Indonesian Presidential Palace, and the interior design of the Dharmawangsa hotel in Jakarta. Jaya & Associates is also involved in several projects in China, Thailand, Sri Lanka, Switzerland, Spain, and the US.

Jaya & Associates

Erlangga V, No. 18
Jakarta 12110

Tel/Fax: (6221) 72792107
E-mail: adminoffice@jaya-associates.com

Jeffrey Budiman

Jeffrey Budiman, born in Bandung in 1962, graduated from Parahyangan Catholic University in his home town in 1987. He worked at the architectural office of Grahacipta Hadiprana for a brief period between 1989 and 1990 before establishing his own firm, J. Budiman Architects. Since then he has worked on various architectural and interior design projects, including a number of shops/showrooms, show units of real estate/housing developments, offices, as well as a club house and a church. His forté, however, lies in the design of houses as evidenced by the more than eighty houses that he has designed to date.

J. Budiman Architects

Mandar XI DE5/9811
Bintaro Jaya Sektor 3A
Jakarta 15225

Tel: (6221) 7365438
Fax: (6221) 7372870
E-mail: jb_architect@cbn.net.id

Judi Wanadi

Judistira (Judi) Wanandi received his Bachelor of Arts in Fine Arts from Tufts University, Medford, Massachusetts, in 1986 and continued his studies in architecture at the University of California, Los Angeles, graduating with a Master of Architecture in 1990. He then worked as an architectural assistant at the offices of Yim Lim Architects in Cambridge, Massachusetts, Carde Killefer Flammang Architects, Santa Monica, and Daniel Chudnovsky AIA Architect, Brentwood, California, before returning to Indonesia. In 1992, together with Cosmas Gozali, he founded Architelier (PT Archindo Ciptakreatif). In 2002, the firm received an IAI Award for Rumah Ganesha, a small resort in Ubud, Bali, and the ICI Award for Rumah Origami, Bandung, and Rumah Opera, Jakarta.

Architelier (PT Archindo Ciptakreatif

Jalan Raya Kebayoran Lama No. 1
Jakarta 11560

Tel: (6221) 5361179/5361180
Fax: (6221) 5356084
E-mail: yudi@architelier.net
Website: www.architelier.net

Kusuma Agustianto

Born in Purwokerto, Central Java, in 1971, Kusuma Agustianto graduated from Parahyangan Catholic University, Bandung, in 1995. The same year, he won first prize in a competition for his plan of the Bandung Railway Station. The following year, he joined the Grahacipta Hadiprana architectural firm where he worked on the designs of villas and residences in West Java, Bali, and Jakarta, as well as a club house in Hanoi, Vietnam. He traveled to Malaysia, Singapore, Thailand, and Australia in 1997, 1998, and 1999 , but it was his excursion to Japan in 2000 with the Forum of Young Indonesian Architects that inspired his recent designs. In 2004, he resigned from Grahacipta Hadiprana and established his own firm, Kusuma Agustianto Architect, the following year.

Grahacipta Hadiprana

Jl. Pangeran Antasari No. 12
Cipete Selatan
Jakarta Selatan 12410

E-mail: gch@cbn.net.id
Website: www.grahaciptahadiprana.com

Patrick Rendradjaja

Patrick Rendradjaja was born in
Banjarmasin, South Kalimantan,
in 1959. After graduating in 1986
with a Master of Science in Architecture (with distinction) from
the Technische Hogeschool Delft,
The Netherlands, he worked as
a draughtsman for Hoogstad
Weeber Van Tilburg Architecten
in Rotterdam and De Architecten
Cie in Amsterdam. On returning to
Indonesia, he worked from 1989
to 1993 as a project architect for
Atelier 6 International Architects,
Jakarta, on a number of hotel projects in Jakarta, Yogyakarta, and
Bali, as well as the Indonesia House
in Amsterdam in association with
Mecanoo Architects. In 1991, he
set up private practice, designing
several houses in Jakarta under
the auspisious of several property
developers. Since 1998, in association with various foreign firms, he
has worked on Multatuli Tower, the
highest apartment in the Netherlands, MGS Tower in Jakarta, and
a number of housing projects in
Zwolle, Hilversum, Vleuten de
Meern, and Amersfoort in the
Netherlands. Since 1999 he has
been Chief Development Officer
of several hotel property developments, including the Paradise
Group and Harris Hotels. He has
lectured at the IAI Forum.

Patrick Rendradjaja, Architect

Kemang Timur IX/28
Jakarta 12730

Tel: (6221) 7190403/816 1102125
Fax: (6221) 7181086
E-mail: patrick@the paradise-
group.com; pat_rendra@hotmail.
com

Sardjono Sani

Born in 1963, B. Sardjono Sani did
his first degree in architecture at
the Parahyangan Catholic University in Bandung before continuing
his studies at the University of
Colorado, Denver, where he ob-
tained his Master of Architecture
in 1990. During his stay in Colorado, he apprenticed with Prof.
J. Darden, the 1986 winner of the
Rome Prize, and became a teaching assistant at the graduate level
studio at the university. Later, he
worked at the Harmonica Office
of Craig, Hodgetts and Fung in
Southern California. After returning to Indonesia, he established
PT Bias Tekno-Art Kreasindo and
has become principal architectural
designer for all projects handled
by the office. Sardjono has been
guest critic at the University of
Indonesia (1994 to present) and
guest lecturer at Tarumanegara
University (1996–7). His design for
his own house in Pondok Indah,
Jakarta, received a citation from
the IAI in 1993.

PT Bias Tekno-Art Kreasindo

Fatmawati Mas Complex kav 324
Jl. Fatmawati Raya 20
Jakarta

Tel: (6221) 7659221/7659222/
7659223
Fax: (6221) 7659220
E-mail: bitek@indo.net.id

Tan Tjiang Ay

Tan Tjiang Ay was born in Central
Java in 1940. He studied at the
Institue of Technology, Bandung,
between 1958 and 1960 and at
Parahyangan Catholic University
of from 1960 to 1968. He was in
private practice between 1968
and 1972, before taking up a partnership with Lampiri Indonesia
Architects for the next eight
years. In 1980, he resumed his
private practice, focusing on the
design of private residences.

Tan Tjian Ay

Jl. Gempol Wetan 113
Bandung 40115

Tel: (6222) 4209476

Ted Sulisto

Ted Sulisto, an interior designer
who was raised in Europe and
educated in the United States,
established Ted Sulisto Design
(TSD) in Jakarta in 1988. The firm
started with renovation work on
small residences, but since then
has grown steadily and been involved in institutional, hospitality,
commercial, retail, and residential
projects in Indonesia as well as in
Europe, America, Australia, and
Brazil. Projects include the Bronze
Room of the National Museum,
Jakarta (1996), the Indonesian
Embassy and Ambassador's Residence, Washington DC (1994), Zan-
zibar Bar & Restaurant, Jakarta
(1996), Rumah Kartanegara Guest
House, Jakarta (2000), Rumah
Sleman Guest House, Yogyakarta
(2001), Prego Bar & Restaurant,
Jakarta (2002), and Madelaine
Brasserie, Arcadia Senayan Plaza,
Jakarta (2005). The firm is well
known for its distinctive blend
of Asian and European design.

Ted Sulisto Design Associates

Satmarindo Buillding
Ground Floor
Jalan Ampera Raya 5
Jakarta 12560

Tel: (6221) 78836682
Fax: (6221) 78837304
E-mail: tsd101@cbn.net.id

Yori Antar

Born in Jakarta in 1962, Yori Antar studied architecture at the University of Indonesia. In 1989, along with a number of recent architectural graduates and students, he formed the Young Indonesian Architects Forum (Arsitek Muda Indonesia—AMI), an informal architectural forum for emerging architects. He has also worked as a freelance architectural photographer, taking pictures for, among others, the Aga Khan Award for Architecture and various publications. Both his architectural work and his photographs have been exhibited and widely published. In 1996, he received the Avcasit Award for an affordable self-developed housing plan for Kupang. Yori has traveled extensively around the world and has great interest in the conservation of historical buildings. In 2004, he was appointed a member of the City Architecture Advisory Committee (Team Penasehat Arsitektur Kota/TPAK).

Han Awal & Partners, Architects

Pondok Pinang Center B-18 & 20
Jl. Ciputat Raya
Jakarta 12310

Tel: (6221) 7509347/7514353
Fax: (6221) 7511726
E-mail: hanawal@attglobal.net

Yusman Siswandi

Designer Yusman Siswandi studied anthropology at Gadjah Mada University in Yogyakarta before moving into the arena of design. In 1987, as the chief designer for Bin House, he won an International Textile Design Contest in Tokyo, Japan. Later, he developed other art craft products and participated in various textile and interior product exhibitions in Tokyo, Osaka, Kyoto, and Kiryu, as well as in Koln, Germany. He has developed designs for houses in Jakarta, Solo, and Bali, and is working on a number of projects in other parts of the world.

Deya Product Design

Jl. Riau No. 2
Jakarta

Tel: (6221) 3152493/3138142
Fax: (6221) 3142792
E-mail: deya@cbn.net.id

1. For information on domestic architecture among the urban middle class, see Amanda Achmadi, "Indonesia: The Emergence of a New Architectural Consciousness of the Urban Middle Classes," in Geoffrey London (ed.), *Houses for the 21st Century*, Sydney: Pesaro Publishing and Singapore: Periplus Editions, 2004, pp. 28–35.

2. For related discussions on this topic, see Philip Goad and Anoma Pieris, *New Directions in Tropical Asian Architecture*, Sydney: Pesaro Publishing and Singapore: Periplus Editions, 2005.

3. For elaboration and historical tracing of orientalism, see Edward Said, *Orientalism: Western Conceptions of the Orient*, London: Penguin, 1995 [1978]. For the tracing of how orientalism implicates architectural studies of Asia, see Stephen Cairns, "The Stone Books of Orientalism," in *Fabrications: The Journal of the Society of Architectural Historians, Australia and New Zealand*, Vol. 11, No. 2, 2001, Kensington, NSW, Australia; and Gülsüm Baydar Nalbantoglu, "(Post)Colonial Architectural Encounters," in Tan Kok Meng (ed.), *Asian Architects Volume 2*, Singapore: Select Books, 2001, pp. 19–27.

4. For critiques on such tendencies, see Anoma Pieris, "Beyond the Vernacular House," in Geoffrey London (ed.), *Houses for the 21st Century*, Sydney: Pesaro Publishing and Singapore: Periplus Editions, 2004, pp. 42–51.

5. See K. Frampton, "Towards a Critical Regionalism: Six Points for an Architecture of Resistance," in H. Foster (ed.), *The Anti-Aesthetic: Essays on Post-Modern Culture*, Seattle: Bay Press, 1983, pp. 16–30.

6. See Liane Lefaivre and Alexander Tzonis, "Tropical Critical Regionalism: Introductory Comments," in Alexander Tzonis, Liane Lefaivre, and Bruno Stagno (eds.), *Tropical Architecture: Critical Regionalism in the Age of Globalization*, Chichester, UK: Wiley-Academy, with Fonds, Prince Claus Fund for Culture and Development, The Netherlands, 2001, pp. 1–13.

7. For a critical examination of architectural regionalist thinking, see A. Colquhoun, "The Concept of Regionalism," in Gülsüm Baydar Nalbantoglu and Wong Chong Thai (eds.), *Postcolonial Space(s)*, New York: Princeton Architectural Press, 1997, pp. 13–23; and G. B. Nalbantoglu, "(Post) Colonial Architectural Encounters," in Tan Kok Meng (ed.), *Asian Architects Volume 2*, Singapore: Select Books, 2001, pp. 19–27.

8. Rem Koolhaas, "Introduction: City of Exacerbated Difference," in Judy Chung Chuihua et al. (eds.), *Great Leap Forward*, Koln: Taschen Gmbh, 2001, pp. 24–9.

9. In revisiting the modern history of architecture in Indonesia, I have relied heavily on Iwan Sudradjat, "A Study of Indonesian Architectural History," unpublished Ph.D. dissertation, Department of Architecture, University of Sydney, 1991.

10. The *pendopo* is the frontmost section of a typical house in the Javanese court. The house is composed by three pavilions: *pendopo*, *pringgitan*, and *dalem*. An open-sided pavilion, the *pendopo* is almost square in plan and has a central structural core of wooden columns that hold up a pyramidal-shaped roof. Its openness signifies its more public function. For critical readings on Karsten and Pont's reworkings of *pendopo* and their propositions in the debate on Indies architecture, see Stephen Cairns, "Re-Surfacing: Architecture, Wayang, and the 'Javanese House'," in Gülsüm Baydar Nalbantoglu and Wong Chong Thai (eds), *Postcolonial Space(s)*, Princeton Architectural Press, New York, 1997, pp. 78–81.

11. For a discussion on the ways of life and forms of residential architecture in the Netherlands East Indies, see Esther Wils, *Wonen in Indië: House and Home in the Dutch East Indies*, Den Haag: Stichting Tong Tong, 2000.

12. See Stephen Cairns, "Re-Surfacing: Architecture, Wayang, and the 'Javanese House'," in Gülsüm Baydar Nalbantoglu and Wong Chong Thai (eds), *Postcolonial Space(s)*, New York: Princeton Architectural Press, 1997, pp. 73–88.

13. See Abidin Kusno, *Behind the Postcolonial: Architecture, Urban Space and Political Cultures in Indonesia*, London: Routledge, 2000, Ch. 2.

14. See Iwan Sudradjat, "A Study of Indonesian Architectural History," unpublished Ph.D. dissertation, Department of Architecture, University of Sydney, 1991, p. 194.

15. For elaborations on different forms and implementations of *kampung* improvement projects during colonial times and post-independency, see Abidin Kusno, *Behind the Postcolonial: Architecture, Urban Space and Political Cultures in Indonesia*, London: Routledge, 2000, pp. 122–43. For reviews of examples of urban house projects designed by Indonesian architects for the country's urban middle class, see Amanda Achmadi, "Indonesia: The Emergence of a New Architectural Consciousness of the Urban Middle Classes," in Geoffrey London (ed.), *Houses for the 21st Century*, Sydney: Pesaro Publishing and Singapore: Periplus Editions, 2004, pp. 28–35, and Amanda Achmadi, "Eko Prawoto," in Philip Goad and Anoma Pieris, *New Directions in Tropical Asian Architecture*, Sydney: Pesaro Publishing and Singapore: Periplus Editions, 2005, pp. 118–27.

16. I am grateful to Jens Eberhardt for his careful reading of early drafts of this article.

acknowledgments

The author and photographer would like to express their gratitude to the many people involved in the publication of this book:

First and foremost, the architects and designers whose exceptional works are the main feature of the book: Adi Purnomo of Studioarsitektur; Ahmad Djuhara of djuhara+djuhara; Albertus Wang of SWiM-CAU; Andra Matin of Andra Matin Architect; Antony Liu and Ferry Ridwan of PT Dwitunggal Mandiri; Baskoro Tedjo of Baskoro Tedjo Associates; Budiman Hendropurnomo and Dicky Hendrasto of Denton Corker Marshall Pty Ltd; Kusuma Agustianto; Faried Masdoeki of Grahacipta Hadiprana; Irianto PH of Antara Design; Jaya Ibrahim of Jaya & Associates; Jeffrey Budiman, Jami Harwig, and Ilham N. of J. Budiman Architects; Judistira Wanandi and Cosmas Gozali of Architelier; Patrick Rendradjaja; Sardjono Sani of PT Bias Tekno-Art Kreasindo; Tan Tjiang Ay; Ted Sulisto of Ted Sulisto Design Associates; Yori Antar of Han Awal & Partners, Architects, and Yusman Siswandi of Deya Product Design.

Very importantly, the home owners who generously opened their beautiful homes to the photography team and without whom this book would not have been possible: Amanda Pritta Wardhani; Ario and Nelly Wibisono; Budi and Lili Taruno; Dadit and Dina Sidharta; Eddy Prayitno and Hetty Herawati, Inke; Iskandar; Prabowo, Rino and Sarah Oestara; Sugiharto; Suta and Yusni; Tantowi Yahya and Dewi; Uran and Shienny The; Yusti Suhendy, as well as those home owners who wish to remain anonymous.

We are also grateful to the following people for their design assistance and for loaning their products for the photography sessions: Aksara and Taksu Jakarta for providing the Accupunto chaise longue for the poolside shots for the Howard House; Anita Boentarman for interior design consultation for the Iskandar Residence; Canna Gallery for providing the paintings for the Howard House; Hendra Gustari of Archipelago, Plaza Senayan, for providing furniture and interior design advice for the Jane House, Steel House, and T House; Kish&Kish for the flower arrangements for the Edi & Hetty Home and Steel House; Millenia Tata Aria for providing the furniture and art for the Iskandar Residence and Tirtawisata House; Nadi Gallery for providing the paintings for the Jane House and Suta House; Pia Alisjahbana for lending her Dede Eri Supria painting for the photography of the Steel House; and Teguh Ostenrik and Bilik3Dharma for providing the paintings and sculptures for the Howard House, T House, and Tirtawisata House.

Amanda Achmadi, who wrote the Introduction.

Reita Malaon, who gathered the initial information on the houses and co-ordinated and styled the photography.

Toshiko Nakamoto, assistant to photographer Masano Kawana.

Nila Yuni, who assisted in the coordination of the photography.

Mariani Suwirya, who converted the architectural drawings into digital format.

F. Cynthia Octavianty, who coordinated various projects and research data.

Nancy M. Sanders, for writing the captions for T House.

As well as many other individuals and entities who have helped with the production of the book.

Addresses of Suppliers

Aksara
Jl. Kemang Raya 8B
Jakarta 12730
Tel: (6221) 7199288
Fax: (6221) 7199287
E-mail: info@aksara.com
Website: www.aksara.com

Archipelago
Plaza Senayan, Ground Floor P1, Palm Gate
Jl. Asia Afrika No. 8
Jakarta 10270
Tel: (6221) 5725144
Fax: (6221) 5725145
E-mail: sales@archipelago-indonesia.com

Canna Gallery
Jl. Boulevard Barat Raya Block LC 6, No. 33-34
Kelapa Gading Permai
Jakarta 14240
Tel: (6221) 4526429/4526430/4522536
Fax: (6221) 4526430
E-mail: canna@cbn.net.id
Website: www.galericanna.com

Millenia Tata Aria
Jl. Bangka Raya 115
Jakarta 12730
Tel: (6221) 7192573, 717922440
Fax: (6221) 7192546
E-mail: millenia@dnet.net.id

Nadi Gallery
Jl. Kembang Indah III
Blok G III No. 4-5 Puri Indah
Jakarta 11610
Tel: (6221) 5818129
Fax: (6221 5805677
E-mail: info@nadigallery.com
Website: www.nadigallery.com

Teguh Ostenrik
Bilik 3Dharma
Jl. Tridharma Utama III/5 RT 009/RW 012
Kampung Pulo Cilandak Barat
Jakarta 124390
Tel: (6221) 7669763
Fax: (6221) 7669762
E-mail: teguhostenrik@gmail.com